THE ONE THING MONEY CAN'T BUY —
THE ONE THING YOU CAN'T
AFFORD TO BE WITHOUT!

CHARACTER

Dr. Jeff Owens

The One Thing Money Can't Buy — The One Thing You Can't Afford To Be Without!

Character

Owens Publications

© 1995

OWENS PUBLICATIONS

P.O. Box 1597
Martinsburg, WV 25402
(304) 229-1338
E-MAIL: sales@owenspublications.com
Web Site: www.owenspublications.com

Cover Design: Harrod Advertising, Highland, Indiana

All Scripture quotations are from the King James Bible.

ISBN 0-9649393-0-4
Library of Congress Catalog Number
95-092777

Sixth Printing

Printed and Bound in the United States of America

Dedication

OF COURSE, THERE ARE no self-made men. Each of us is merely the sum total of what everyone else has invested in us.

If I were to dedicate this book to all who have contributed to it and its author, the book itself could not contain all the names. Therefore, I will choose one to whom I feel deeply indebted and one whom I also deeply love — my wife Schery. This book would not have been possible if it were not for her faithful backing, encouragement, and undying support.

I only wish that this dedication could be written in the stars for all to see. She would then receive but a fraction of her much-deserved praise.

About the Author

DR. JEFF OWENS IS a four-time college graduate. He and his wife, Schery, have been married since 1981. They have four wonderful children and one daughter-in-law. Dr. Owens has been preaching since 1976. He is currently the pastor of the Shenandoah Bible Baptist Church in Martinsburg, West Virginia. He was, for years, a faculty member at Hyles-Anderson College and Seminary in Crown Point, Indiana. He also served as an assistant pastor for 14 years to the late Dr. Jack Hyles at the First Baptist Church of Hammond, Indiana, "the World's Largest Sunday School," averaging 20,000 people per Sunday.

Dr. Jeff Owens has preached tens of thousands of sermons and has seen over 100,000 people profess Christ as Saviour as a result. (Dr. Owens frequently speaks across the country as well as abroad in revival meetings, youth and marriage conferences and in a variety of other meetings.)

He is a Bible-believing, God-fearing, patriotic American. Brother Owens believes that Christian character is the great need of the hour in our country.

Acknowledgments

T̲HANK YOU TO THE following people for teaching me about character by their example:

- Mr. Delbert Rittenhouse
- Mrs. Judy Warfel
- Mr. and Mrs. Eugene Owens, Jr.
- Mr. Al Thompson
- Dr. Jack Hyles
- Mr. Dave Eley
- Dr. Ray Young

T̲HANK YOU TO THE following people for helping me to compile the contents of this book:

- Mrs. Becky Ramsey
- Mrs. Linda Stubblefield
- Mrs. Martha Gilbert
- Mrs. Renée Parris
- Mrs. Karen Kalapp

Table of Contents

	Foreword .... *xi*
	Recommendation of the Author .... *xiii*
1	*Character and How to Achieve It* 1
2	*Character Quotes and Comments* 7
3	*Character and People with Character* 17
4	*Character and Our Employment* 39
5	*Character and the Bible, a Book Full of Good Workers* 47
6	*Character and Our Sleep Habits* 61
7	*The Ten Commandments of Character* 71
8	*Character and Having a Good Name to Reflect It* 73
9	*Character and Our God, a Perfect Example* 81
10	*Character and Seeking Counsel* 91
11	*Character and Reading the Bible* 97
12	*Character and Our Burdens* 103
13	*Character and Diligence* 113
14	*Character and Laziness* 119
15	*Character and Our Need to Be Accountable* 125
16	*Character and When Our Flesh Is Weak* 129
17	*Character and Developing It in Our Children* 135
18	*Character and Respect for Our Elders* 139
19	*Character and Having the Sense to Avoid What You Cannot Resist* 147
20	*Character and One of the Surest Ways Not to Get It* .. 155
21	*Character and Our Strength* 161
22	*Character and Salvation* 169
23	*Character and the Goal of Godly Leadership* 173
24	*Character and Being a Martyr for Your Marriage* 183
25	*Character and Our Eating Habits* 191
26	*Character and Our Money* 195
27	*Character and the Importance of Finishing What You Start* 199

Foreword

FOR OVER THIRTY YEARS, I have had the opportunity to observe and learn from Dr. Jeff Owens. I have watched him take people who were seemingly hopeless, without direction, and purposeless in life and patiently work with them and teach them how to develop character within themselves. By being strong in self-discipline himself, he has instilled in many a truly disciplined life full of character by means of his preaching and teaching.

Being under my watchful eye as his wife for over twenty-four years, I have had the privilege of seeing him live every word of this book in his everyday home life, even when it was not easy. His consistency of character has nurtured security in my life and the lives of our four children.

Surely, anyone who comes into contact with him is being taught character as he teaches continuously with his own life. I am proud to be the wife of such a man.

– Mrs. Jeffery (Schery) Owens

Recommendation of the Author
by Dr. Jack Hyles

THIS EPISTLE IS NOT needed by those who know Dr. Jeff Owens. To know him is to know character and integrity. To those who do not know Jeff Owens, this book will be only a window through which one can look into his life. It will be a shadow of the man, but that window and that shadow will give a strong impression as to the man Jeff Owens. To know him and to see the epistle of his life is best. To those who do not have that privilege, but who read this manuscript, this will, of course, be second best but still a great blessing.

For years I have read the epistle of his life not written with pen and ink. Now I recommend to you this window and shadow. You will be a better person because you have read it.

> "The saddest thought that I have as I prepare this book on character is that the average person who will begin to read it will not even have the character to read it all the way to the end. I hope that I am not describing you with this statement."
>
> – Dr. Jeff Owens

char•ac•ter (kăr' ĭk-tər) *n.*

1. A person marked by notable qualities or trains of consistency

2. Reputation

3. Moral excellence and firmness: *a man of sound character*

Chris•tian char•ac•ter (krĭs' chən kăr' ĭk-tər) *n.*

The subconscious doing of right or moral excellence, firmness, and consistency for Christ

Chapter 1

Character
and
How to Achieve It

THE BIBLE SAYS IN John 6:1-15, *"After these things Jesus went over the sea of Galilee, which is the sea of Tiberias. And a great multitude followed him, because they saw his miracles which he did on them that were diseased. And Jesus went up into a mountain, and there he sat with his disciples. And the passover, a feast of the Jews, was nigh. When Jesus then lifted up his eyes, and saw a great company come unto him, he saith unto Philip, Whence shall we buy bread, that these may eat? And this he said to prove him: for he himself knew what he would do. Philip answered him, Two hundred pennyworth of bread is not sufficient for them, that every one of them may take a little. One of his disciples, Andrew, Simon Peter's brother, saith unto him, There is a lad here, which hath five barley loaves, and two small fishes: but what are they among so many? And Jesus said, Make the men sit down. Now there was much grass in the place. So the men sat down, in number about five thousand. And Jesus took the loaves; and when he had given thanks, he distributed to the disciples, and the disciples to them that were set down; and likewise of the fishes as much as they would. When they were filled, he said unto his disciples, Gather up the fragments that remain, that nothing be lost. Therefore they gathered them together, and filled twelve baskets with the fragments of the five barley loaves, which remained over and above unto them that had eaten. Then those men, when they had seen the miracle that Jesus did, said, This is of a truth that prophet that should come into the world. When Jesus therefore perceived that they would come and take him by force, to make him a king, he departed again into a mountain himself alone."*

These verses give an account of the very famous feeding of the 5,000 by Jesus. A little lad gave his lunch of five barley loaves and two small fishes, and the Bible says that Jesus blessed it, brake it into pieces, and distributed it to the disciples, who gave it to the hungry people. After everyone had eaten his fill, Jesus instructed the disciples to gather the excess, and 12 baskets of fragments of barley loaves were left. The 5,000 saw a great miracle!

Look again at John 6:15 which says, *"When Jesus therefore perceived that they would come and take him by force to make him a king, he departed again into a mountain himself alone."* After the people had seen the miracle, they wanted to take Jesus by force to make him a king. The Bible says that Jesus perceived their intentions, so he slipped off into a mountain alone.

You might wonder, "Why? Why did Jesus leave when the people wanted Him to be their king? That would seem to be a great honor." I believe I can answer that very simply — He could not become what He already was! Jesus was already the King of kings!

Please let me share some principles I have learned from the miracle of the feeding of the 5,000.

1. Man cannot force Jesus to be a king. Jesus is *the* King already! In Genesis 1:1 the Bible says, *"In the beginning God created the heaven and the earth."* This verse says He was the Creator. In the account of the feeding of the 5,000 in John 6, we find man, a limited, created being, saying to the Creator that Jesus ought to be made a king.

Psalm 90:2 says, *"Before the mountains were brought forth, or ever thou hadst formed the earth and the world, even from everlasting to everlasting, thou art God."* Jesus is the Eternal One. In John 6 we find man, who has limited days, wanting to force the Eternal One to become what He already was!

Proverbs 15:3 tells us, *"The eyes of the LORD are in every place, beholding the evil and the good."* Here is the All-knowing One being told by some uneducated humans that they were going to make Him into a king. Man's finite mind cannot even comprehend the greatness of God.

Psalm 93:5 states, *"Thy testimonies are very sure: holiness becometh thine house, O LORD, for ever."* He is the Pure One and the Just One being told by a group of sinful men that He ought to be made a king.

Psalm 95:3-5 says, *"For the LORD is a great God, and a great King above all gods. In his hand are the deep places of the earth: the strength of the hills is his also. The sea is his, and he made it: and his hands formed the dry land."* The Owner of everything was being told by a group of people, who borrow the very air they breathe, that they were going to force Him to become a king.

Psalm 139:7-10 says, *"Whither shall I go from thy spirit? or whither shall I flee from thy presence? If I ascend up into heaven, thou art there: if I make my bed in hell, behold, thou art there. If I take the wings of the morning, and dwell in the uttermost parts of the sea; Even there shall thy hand lead me, and thy right hand shall hold me."* Jesus is the Omnipresent One being told by man, who can only be in one place at one time, that Jesus ought to be a king.

2. Jesus is already a king. Psalm 24:7 says, *"Lift up your heads, O ye gates; and be ye lift up, ye everlasting doors; and the King of glory shall come in."* This verse is speaking of Jesus as being the King of glory.

Psalm 10:16a states, *"The LORD is King for ever and ever."* This verse tells us that Jesus is the Eternal King. I Timothy 6:15 says, *"Which in his times he shall shew, who is the blessed and only Potentate, the King of kings, and Lord of lords."* He is the King of kings.

3. Your character should force you to become a servant. Instead of wanting to force Jesus to become the king He already was, the people should have realized they needed to force themselves to become servants to Him. He will not force you to serve Him. Becoming a servant will require changing one's attitude. Some people are waiting for Jesus to force them to serve Him. Some people are waiting for Jesus to make Himself King in their lives. Forcing is not something that Jesus does. If anybody is going to force you to do right, it is the person who puts on your shoes every morning. If you want Jesus to be the King of your life, then you must force yourself to become a servant.

The problem is that many are not willing to be what they are supposed to be. Change what needs to be corrected so you can become a servant. We are not qualified to be a servant without making needed changes.

4. For success, add reading God's Word and following the prompting of God's Spirit to build character. When you were saved, Jesus gave you the two tools you needed to become that servant. In essence God said, "I'm going to give you a tool box, and in that tool box I will put a couple of things that will help you to become a servant."

> a. **He gave you His Word.** Psalm 119:28b says, *"Strengthen thou me according unto thy word."* The Bible says that before you were saved you would not have an understanding of the Bible. But after salvation, God gave you an understanding of His Book. One way God gives you strength to serve is through reading, studying, and meditating on His Word.
>
> b. **He gave you His Spirit.** The second tool in that tool box is His Spirit. Ephesians 1:13 tells us, *"... After that ye believed, ye were sealed with that holy Spirit of promise."* The very day you were saved, God gave you the Holy Spirit of God to help you understand His Word so you could have the strength to serve, guidance to serve, and encouragement to serve.

5. Christian character is the subconscious doing of right. This means we do *right by reflex.* However, before anyone can instinctively do right, he must first consciously do right.

Let me explain by means of a very elementary example. When I was a little baby, my mama would hold me in her arms and say, "Jeffery." I would look up and think, "Who is this Jeffery?" I had never before heard my name. Mama would say the word over and over again, "Jeffery ... Jeffery ... Jeffery ... Jeff ... Jeff ... Jeff ...." When I was older and when I got into trouble, Mama said, "Jeffery

Allen." That's because Allen is my middle name, and any time your mama uses your middle name, you know that you are in trouble! I heard "Jeffery Allen" used quite frequently! Now, I can be in a room with hundreds of people, hear the name "Jeff," and I respond without thinking. So does every other guy in the world with the name "Jeff."

My name had been driven into my mind, and now I intuitively react to hearing the name "Jeff." It is a subconscious reaction that came as a response to conscious training. In much the same way, Christian character is the subconscious doing of right. However, before any person will subconsciously do right, he must program himself to **consciously** do right. We are to do right because it is right to do.

6. My character forces me to read my Bible. Reading the Bible is not always easy for anyone. Reading the Bible consistently is a challenge for anyone. You might say, "Oh, Brother Owens, I thought that every Christian loved and enjoyed the Bible all the time. I thought that I was the only person in the world who had to force himself to read his Bible." No, there's not a person reading this book on character who does not force himself at times to read his Bible. That is because the Devil does not want you to spend time in the Word of God.

Why do I force myself to read the Bible? It is because it is right. I read the Bible because it's right; and if I read the Bible because it is right, eventually it is going to become a part of me. I want to become a servant to my King, and then my King will bless me with enjoyment in reading my Bible. About half of the time, I do not enjoy reading my Bible.

When I have made this statement publicly, I have had people say something like, "Brother Owens, do you mean that in six months out of twelve, you don't like reading your Bible?" No! Let me explain: During my Bible reading time, I usually don't enjoy the first half of it. But I force myself to continue reading my Bible. I can be reading along and will think, "I don't like doing this." About halfway through my time set aside for Bible reading, suddenly something happens, and I begin to enjoy it! One thing that happens is that I begin to realize how much I need the Word of God. **I force myself to do right.** I do right because it is right to do, not because it is easy or convenient. You are just like everybody else; as you develop character in the area of your Bible reading, it soon becomes more pleasant.

    7. My character forces me to pray. I force myself to pray. Praying is not easy for anyone. I believe most people would tell you that it is a challenge to pray. In all honesty, I hate to admit there are times when I don't enjoy praying. As a matter of fact, about half the time I don't enjoy it. I don't enjoy the first half of my prayer time. I force myself to go to prayer; then, all of a sudden, about halfway through my prayer time, something happens. I say, "Lord, I really need You today. I didn't realize how badly. Oh, God, help me; God, I need you. I'm sorry I acted that way. Lord, bless me now ...." But you see, I never would have gotten there had I not forced myself to do right first. It took **character** to get me the blessing.

    8. My character forces me to go soul winning. I force myself to go soul winning. There are times I don't like to go soul winning. Do you know what I think when I go soul winning? My first thought when I am knocking on a door is, "I hope they're not here." Sound familiar?! It's hard to go door-to-door and talk to people you have never met and tell them about Jesus. About half the time I don't enjoy my soul winning — the first half of my soul winning. Once I win someone to Christ, suddenly something happens! Just let me get one person saved and I am ready to go soul winning 24 hours a day!

    In conclusion, it may seem that achieving character is pretty cut-and-dried. It is. Do you want character? Force yourself to do right. If you don't want character, just go ahead and do what you want. If you want character, let the Word of God guide you. Try to always do what the Bible says — whether you like it or not — and you **will** develop this intangible called Christian character.

    "Are there any shortcuts, Brother Owens?" "Sorry, no shortcuts!" "Is there a simpler way?" "Sorry, there is no simpler way."

    If you want Christian character, you seek to have it. God won't force character on you, nor will He force Himself on you. You can't force him to be King. However, you could force yourself to get character.

Chapter 2

Character Quotes and Comments

GREAT MEN REALIZE THE importance of possessing character. The following 24 quotes are by famous men who are known for possessing an inordinate amount of character. I want to apply each of these philosophies to my life.

To know the will of God is the greatest knowledge. To find the will of God is the greatest discovery. To do the will of God is the greatest achievement.
— Dr. George W. Truett

We are taught when we study our Bible that we will know what God wants us to do with our lives. We then search to find the place where God would like us to do what He wants us to do. Then, we ought to start that work immediately!

The what of the will of God is most important.
— Dr. Jack Hyles

There are people who are in the right place geographically, but they are not doing the right thing. Therefore, what good is it to be in the right place doing the wrong thing? Anywhere you go could be the will of God as long as you are doing what He wants you to do.

Happy is the man who dreams dreams and is willing to pay the price to make them come true. — Unknown

Do you realize that if you have a great dream, you have something most people do not possess? Go ahead and dream. You must then open your eyes, wake up, and do something about your dream because nothing is ever accomplished by dreaming. I often wonder if the part that dreaming takes in life is not the organization that takes place in the mind while one plans to be a success for God. Are you willing to pay the price of just being diligent and working hard to see your dreams come true?

I am only one, but I am one. I can't do everything, but I can do something. And what I can do I ought to do, and what I ought to do, by the grace of God, I will do.
— D. L. Moody

The best carpenter is not the one who makes the prettiest sound when the hammer hits the nails or has the most graceful stroke with the saw. The best carpenter is the one who builds the best house. — Dr. Jack Hyles

Some people believe they must swing the hammer "just right" as they work. Some laborers believe they have to stroke the saw through the wood "just right." They spend so much time doing things "just right" to make themselves look good that nothing is ever built.

CHARACTER QUOTES AND COMMENTS

❖ ❖ ❖

The test of your character is what it takes to stop you.
— **Dr. Bob Jones, Sr.**

In your mind, underline the words "stop you." Ask yourself what it takes to stop you. Often something petty, childish, and juvenile causes us to quit. This proves that we are petty, childish, and juvenile.

❖ ❖ ❖

What you do before sunup determines whether you have victory before sundown. — **Brother Lester Roloff**

If you want to see more victories, you ought to get up a little earlier in the morning. When you get up at the last minute and try to get all your responsibilities done, you are setting yourself up for failure. I believe that to sleep one minute more than what your body actually needs or to eat a bite more than what your body needs for energy is sinful. Anything done in excess usually is not good. Walk with God before sunrise, and He will be with you all day long.

True character, when it is instilled in the lives of young people, will find the talent necessary to perform the task.
— **Dr. Jack Hyles**

Once you have godly character, everything else is made available to you. If you determine that you are going to learn to be on time, work hard, be diligent, be honest, and have integrity, I cannot think of anything worth having in life that could not be made available to you. Your talents will not earn everything for you. The highest reward for a man's toil is not what he receives for that work, but what he becomes by the sweat of his brow. Too often we think, "The great reward is what I receive!" No, the great reward is what you become!

CHARACTER

My people's great need is my own personal holiness.
— Unknown

People need to see the holiness of God lived out in the lives of man. I do not know if there is anything much more important than for a Christian to live a holy life. Learn to be holy. Do not be average in the way that you are living for God.

You can borrow brains, but you can't borrow character.
— Dr. Bob Jones, Sr.

Please use the formal education God has allowed you to have to be productive for Him. Many want an education to get out of doing work, when the actual purpose of being formally educated is to accomplish more work.

The measure of a man's real character is what he would do if no one would find out. **— Unknown**

Do you know who or what you are? The real you is what you do when you are alone. Too many people spend too much time working on the outward appearance when they ought to be doing something about the inside. *"For the LORD seeth not as man seeth; for man looketh on the outward appearance, but the LORD looketh on the heart."* (I Samuel 16:7b) It is not what a man has or even what he does that directly expresses his worth; it is what he is.

I've never seen a man made by a crisis. The crisis just

exposed the man for what he already was.
— Dr. Bob Jones, Sr.

We make excuses and say, "Had I not been under those circumstances, I wouldn't have behaved that way!" You shouldn't have been under the circumstances; you should have been living above them. I will promise you that the inception of the crisis proves what you actually are. Face yourself. We can thank God for crisis times because we are given an opportunity to see how weak we really are as well as the chance to grow.

Success is to be measured not so much by the position that one has reached in life, but by the obstacles which he has overcome while trying to succeed.
— Booker T. Washington

Character is doing right without regard to inward desire, outward pressure, or eventual outcome. — Dr. Bill Rice

There are two freedoms: the false — where one is free to do what he likes; and the true — where he is free to do what he ought to do. — Unknown

Success is obedience to the unknown revealed will of God, regardless of the consequences. — Unknown

CHARACTER

Men are always wanting to do some great thing; let them overcome themselves, for this is the greatest conquest.
— **Unknown**

The yoke of Jesus is always easy for the true sheep, but it will rub a goat's neck raw. — **Joe Henry Hankins**

You attract what you are, not what you want.
— **Dr. Curtis Hutson**

I've heard people say, "Well, anybody could build a great church if they had a great staff to help them." Maybe so, but not just every man could attract a great staff. You will attract someone who is what you are, not what you want. Do you want to marry someone who is just like you?

Christians are the only people in the world who know where they came from, where they are going, and what they are supposed to be doing while they are here.
— **Dr. Bob Jones, Sr.**

The happiest folks in the world are not the ones who have the most, but they are the ones who want the least.
— **Unknown**

You have a choice in life. You can decide that you are going to be happy with what you have, or you can go ahead and be unhappy because you want something more. There will always be something

CHARACTER QUOTES AND COMMENTS

else to want. Be content. Paul wrote in Philippians 4:11b, *"In whatsoever state I am, therewith to be content."*

Character is more important than talent, for character will seek talent, and talent ofttimes will flee character.
— Dr. Jack Hyles

Somehow we get the idea that if we can develop certain talents we have "arrived." What you need to have is *character*. If you get character, there is no talent that is unavailable to you.

I don't care how loud a brother shouts and how high he jumps, just so he walks straight when he comes down.
— Uncle "Bud" Robinson

This quote reminds me of a story I once heard about a well-promoted and well-planned boxing match. The arena where the match was to be held was packed full of people with standing room only. Suddenly, the normal roar of the crowd heightened to a deafening pitch when one of the boxers came from the locker room in one of the back corners. This strong bull of a man had great big, massive arms. He was wearing red, white, and blue boxing shorts and had a silk robe of the same colors draped over his shoulders. He came down the aisle toward the boxing ring, punching and jabbing a make-believe opponent, and the sweat was already pouring off him.

Normally, a manager puts one foot on the bottom rope of the ring, and he grabs the others and lifts them so the boxer can step through into the ring. Not this guy — he went to his corner and with one vertical leap, vaulted over the ropes and hit the floor of the ring, still punching, jabbing, and sparring with his imaginary opponent. The crowd was going crazy!

When the excitement dulled a bit, from another door came a

CHARACTER

plain-looking man with a simple-looking robe. When the opponent walked out the door, he looked at the center of the ring where the man in red, white, and blue was still punching, jabbing, and sweating and creating excitement. The plain man just calmly fastened his eyes on his opponent and quietly walked toward the ring. When he got to the ring, the manager (as is traditional) lifted the ropes, allowing him to step through, and he calmly walked to his corner. There he very quietly took off his robe.

The official called the boxers to the center of the ring. The plain man calmly walked out. The other man jumped from his corner out to the center. The plain man just stared at his opponent while the animated boxer glared back. The official said, "No hittin' below the belt. Go to your corner. When you hear the bell, come out boxing."

When the bell rang, the wild man took the center of the ring in one leap. The plain man calmly walked out to the center of the ring. The crowd was going crazy! The unforeseen happened suddenly with the sound of one blow — THUMMMP! Down went blustery red, white, and blue — knocked out cold! The plain man turned around, walked back to his corner, put on his robe, and stepped out of the ring. His manager said, "I don't care how much smoke they blow going into the ring; you just always be the man coming out."

What did this boxing story have to do with being a good Christian? I don't care how much you whoop and holler or how much of a commotion you make. You just walk straight because you don't need to prove to anyone that you are somebody. Just make sure you always do right.

It's a great deal easier to do that which God gives us to do, no matter how hard it is, than to face the responsibilities of not doing it. — Dr. J. R. Miller

Doing what is right is easier to do than to face what you must face for not doing your duty. It is much easier to do right now than to face God someday for not doing right. Yes, winning souls may be hard, but you are better off to go soul winning now than later to have another's blood on your hands.

You might say, "It's hard to pay my bills." I would rather go through the struggle of paying a bill than to face the fact that my reputation is ruined and people think I am dishonest.

Some may say, "It's hard to stay married!" Well, maybe it is. However, I can attest by watching the tangled lives of loved ones that it is harder to be divorced!

Many of life's failures are men who did not realize how close they were to success when they gave up.
— **Unknown**

Many of you do not realize that just one more step may hold the answer. Just take one more step; go a little further. I wonder how many men, who would have been great men, quit one day before God really did something big in their lives.

Don't you think the Devil fights the hardest a couple of minutes before the victory? The Devil knows and realizes he has little time to work his deceit. Some of you allow the Devil to prematurely stop you on the road to success. We can only take one step at a time, so just take the next step.

In conclusion, I trust these statements will stir your heart as they did mine when I latched onto them. Latch onto a truth, and do something with your life for God.

Chapter 3

Character and People with Character

THE ATTRIBUTES OF A **LEADER** WHO POSSESSES CHARACTER:

1. The character of a leader causes him to lead himself before he attempts to lead others.
2. The character of a leader insists that he not ask anything of his people that he himself would not be willing to do.
3. The character of a leader requires that he not use his people to benefit himself or his work; instead, he uses his work and himself to benefit his people.
4. The character of a leader will cause him to be first on the job and the last to leave.
5. The character of a leader is proven by his ability to create in the hearts of his people a desire to follow. This followship is not achieved by intimidation or fear.
6. The character of a leader realizes his people are to be trained and prepared, not terrorized.
7. The character of a leader demands that he set the example in the area of giving.
8. The character of a leader includes much organization on his part.
9. The character of a leader is demonstrated in preventive maintenance rather than in breakdown maintenance.

CHARACTER

10. The character of a leader causes him to control himself while others are often out of control.
11. The character of a leader is demonstrated when the leader has been knocked down. Unbeknownst to his people, he is attempting to get up himself while at the same time he is busy helping someone else get up.
12. The character of a leader believes that he should not be distressed; but, if ever he is, he works diligently while distressed.
13. The character of a leader insists that he be more concerned about the condition of his organization than in the position of his organization at the polls.
14. The character of a leader is never completely developed.
15. The character of a leader can be determined on his belief that the doing of right is never a sacrifice.
16. The character of a leader says, "Anything worth doing is worth doing right."
17. The character of a leader says, "Anything not worth doing right is not worth doing."
18. The character of a leader says, "To save time, I will do it right the first time."
19. The character of a leader says, "I believe that character can be developed in each and every one of my people, and I must be a partaker in that development."
20. The character of a leader says, "I would rather attempt a good thing and fail than to attempt nothing and succeed."
21. The character of a leader says, "When I see injustices, I must work long enough and hard enough to earn the right to be in charge of that unjust situation. Then I may correct it."
22. The character of a leader is evident to those around him, but not quite as evident to himself.
23. The character of a leader is determined not so much by what he gets in life as by what he has become in life.
24. The character of a leader is as such that he does not arise to an occasion, but that occasions arise for him.
25. The character of a leader allows him never to be found under the circumstances, but he is always on top of the circumstances.

CHARACTER AND PEOPLE WITH CHARACTER

26. The character of a leader will cause him to enjoy it when one of his followers excels him in any given area. He considers this his own success.
27. The character of a leader says, "I do not care who receives the credit. I just care that the job is done well and right."
28. The character of a leader will not allow him to sacrifice tomorrow's stability on the altar of today's success. He has long-term love and plans for all that he does.
29. The character of a leader determines to be an inch closer to the solution on Tuesday than he was on Monday — at least an inch closer.
30. The character of a leader is seen clearly in the way God leads His people.

Note: After reading this material, a leader with character will spend more time developing his own character than he will pointing out the character flaws of others.

THE ATTRIBUTES OF A **FOLLOWER** WHO POSSESSES CHARACTER:

1. A follower with character is more concerned with being a good follower than if his leader is being a good leader.
2. A follower with character works hard to please his leader.
3. A follower with character is a need-filler.
4. A follower with character does not have to understand why; it is his choice to do the job.
5. A follower with character is willing to change midstream and go in a different direction if the leader requests it.
6. A follower with character does not need to receive recognition for everything he does.
7. A follower with **real** character wants his leader to get credit.
8. A follower with character desires to build his leader.
9. A follower with character does not show up at the last minute.
10. A follower with character will someday be a leader with character.

CHARACTER

11. A follower with character understands when the leader has a difficult or bad day.
12. A follower with character serves at times and expects nothing in return.
13. A follower with character who does not believe a victory can be won should keep quiet while his leaders win the victory.
14. A follower with character needs to realize a man's intensity may determine the immensity of the tasks given by God or man.
15. A follower with character understands that climbing the ladder of success means using his hands, not keeping them in his pockets.

Note: After reading this material, a follower with character will spend more time developing his own character than he will pointing out the character flaws of others.

THE ATTRIBUTES OF A **FATHER** WHO POSSESSES CHARACTER:

1. A father with character will be concerned that his children possess character.
2. A father with character will be concerned that his children know they have a father who gives both quality and quantity time.
3. A father with character will provide for the monetary needs of his children.
4. A father with character will be an example of character for his children.
5. A father with character will clean up his plate as a good example.
6. A father with character will teach his children to be on time by example.
7. A father with character will teach his children to work hard by example.
8. A father with character will express love to his wife so his children may know how a father should behave toward his spouse.

9. A father with character will express his love, gratitude, and concern for his parents so his children will love their grandparents, as well as learn how to care for their future aged parents.
10. A father with character disciplines his children for their good, not for his own gratification.

Note: *After reading this material, a father with character will spend more time developing his own character than he will pointing out the character flaws of others.*

THE ATTRIBUTES OF A **HUSBAND** WHO POSSESSES CHARACTER:

1. A husband with character will love his wife and express it in many ways, including the use of words.
2. A husband with character will provide for his wife.
3. A husband with character will help his wife when she falls behind with her housework instead of complaining.
4. A husband with character will be faithful to his wife, whether or not she is faithful to him.
5. A husband with character will meet his wife's emotional needs by saying "I love you" in a variety of ways.
6. A husband with character will love his wife *"as Christ also loved the church, and gave himself for it."*
7. A husband with character will see to it that he supports his wife and that it is not necessary that she supports him.
8. A husband with character who expects his wife to help support the family in turn will help her with the housework.
9. A husband with character will remember his wife is the weaker vessel and will protect her.
10. A husband with character will lead his wife rather than dictate to her.

Note: *After reading this material, a husband with character will spend more time developing his own character than he will pointing out the character flaws of others.*

CHARACTER

THE ATTRIBUTES OF A **WIFE** WHO POSSESSES CHARACTER:

1. A wife with character will be in submission to her husband, even if she feels he is not worthy of her submission.
2. A wife with character will love her husband.
3. A wife with character will do all that she can to build up her husband rather than to tear him down.
4. A wife with character will attempt to have supper for her husband, whether or not he is home on time.
5. A wife with character will clean the house as many times as is necessary.
6. A wife with character will not go to bed at night with dirty dishes in the sink.
7. A wife with character is as concerned about the cleanliness of the places in the house that cannot be seen as she is concerned with the places of the house that can be seen.
8. A wife with character realizes that she first should serve her husband and not another's husband.
9. A wife with character shows thankfulness to her husband.
10. A wife with character keeps herself nice, even if her husband does not.

Note: After reading this material, a wife with character will spend more time developing her own character than she will pointing out the character flaws of others.

THE ATTRIBUTES OF A **MOTHER** WHO POSSESSES CHARACTER:

1. A mother with character will help develop character in her children.

CHARACTER AND PEOPLE WITH CHARACTER

2. A mother with character will teach her daughter how to can vegetables, whether or not it is cheaper, easier, or more convenient.
3. A mother with character will teach her daughter to sew.
4. A mother with character will be an example to her daughter of how to be a good wife.
5. A mother with character will understand that a microwave is a convenience, not a necessity, and that the daughter and children should be taught the same.
6. A mother with character makes homemade cookies.
7. A mother with character does not throw away the socks because they have holes, but darns and repairs the socks.
8. A mother with character irons even the permanent-press clothes.
9. A mother with character makes home a pleasant place by being a pleasant person.
10. A mother with character takes the time to kiss her child's "boo-boo."

Note: After reading this material, a mother with character will spend more time developing her own character than she will pointing out the character flaws of others.

THE ATTRIBUTES OF A **SON** WHO POSSESSES CHARACTER:

1. A son with character obeys his father.
2. A son with character obeys his mother.
3. A son with character will express his love to his parents in a variety of ways.
4. A son with character will work diligently at school for his family's namesake.
5. A son with character will realize that when he is late his family suffers because of it.
6. A son with character will defend his father.

CHARACTER

7. A son with character will fight for his mother.
8. A son with character will grow up, leave home, support himself, and not depend on Mommy and Daddy for the rest of his life.
9. A son with character will learn to get up in the morning without his parents telling him to get up.
10. A son with character will clean his room when he has been told.
11. A son with character eventually will not need to be told to clean his room.
12. A son with character will polish his shoes.
13. A son with character will learn to pay his bills on time.
14. A son with character will not ask Mom and Dad to give him everything he wants, but he will learn to earn his own keep.
15. A son with character will protect his sister.

Note: *After reading this material, a son with character will spend more time developing his own character than he will pointing out the character flaws of others.*

THE ATTRIBUTES OF A **DAUGHTER** WHO POSSESSES CHARACTER:

1. A daughter with character will learn to obey her mother.
2. A daughter with character will learn to obey her father.
3. A daughter with character will be helpful around the house.
4. A daughter with character will not run from the responsibility of washing the dishes.
5. A daughter with character will be a need-filler, not a need-creator.
6. A daughter with character will learn to sew.
7. A daughter with character will learn to be satisfied with a secondhand dress.
8. A daughter with character will earn her keep at home.
9. A daughter with character will attempt to have a good, moral, clean name for her parents' sake.

10. A daughter with character will learn how to meet the needs of her father; therefore, she will learn to meet the needs of her future husband.
11. A daughter with character ought to encourage her parents.
12. A daughter with character will wait to bear children until after she is married.
13. A daughter with character will dress in a moral fashion.
14. A daughter with character will strive to learn to someday be a good mother.
15. A daughter with character will learn to cook and keep house.

Note: After reading this material, a daughter with character will spend more time developing her own character than she will pointing out the character flaws of others.

THE ATTRIBUTES OF AN **EMPLOYER** WHO POSSESSES CHARACTER:

1. An employer with character pays an honest day's wage for an honest day's work.
2. An employer with character trains the people to do the job so they can live up to his expectations.
3. An employer with character is as concerned with his employee as he is with his product.
4. An employer with character leads and does not dictate.
5. An employer with character gives an employee job security.
6. An employer with character rewards an employee's advancement.
7. An employer with character is a good example of the work ethic before his employees.
8. An employer with character understands that no one is perfect.
9. An employer with character has reasonable expectations.
10. An employer with character is as honest with his employees as he would want them to be with him.

CHARACTER

Note: After reading this material, an employer with character will spend more time developing his own character than he will pointing out the character flaws of others.

THE ATTRIBUTES OF AN **EMPLOYEE** WHO POSSESSES CHARACTER:

1. An employee with character comes to work on time, every time.
2. An employee with character does not stop work early for his break.
3. An employee with character gets back from his lunch break on time.
4. An employee with character does not quit early at the end of the day.
5. An employee with character admits when he makes mistakes that cost the employer money.
6. An employee with character should work as diligently as he would want someone to work for him.
7. An employee with character should be grateful for his employer.
8. An employee with character should learn to say "thank you."
9. An employee with character does not have to have a union to prove that he has personal character.
10. An employee with character gets to work a few minutes early.
11. An employee with character is willing to work a few minutes after quitting time, if necessary.
12. An employee with character is willing to do any task necessary.
13. An employee with character never criticizes the employer.
14. An employee with character realizes that if he were such a "hot-shot" he would be running the company; since he is not, he needs to do his job willingly.
15. An employee with character is clean.

Note: After reading this material, an employee with character will spend more time developing his own character than he will pointing out the character flaws of others.

CHARACTER AND PEOPLE WITH CHARACTER

THE ATTRIBUTES OF A **GUEST** WHO POSSESSES CHARACTER:

1. A guest who has character will make his own bed.
2. A guest who has character will attempt to pay his own way.
3. A guest who has character will help to clean off the table at the conclusion of the meal.
4. A guest who has character will be concerned about whether or not he should wear shoes on the carpeting.
5. A guest who has character will not wear out his welcome.
6. A guest who has character will not make requests that cause his host's job to be more complicated.
7. A guest who has character should forget he is a guest and try to become a host.
8. A guest who has character will be grateful and express his gratefulness by word and by note.
9. A guest who has character will not assume anything.
10. A guest who has character will try to be a need-filler and not a need-creator.

Note: After reading this material, a guest with character will spend more time developing his own character than he will pointing out the character flaws of others.

THE ATTRIBUTES OF A **GRANDPARENT** WHO POSSESSES CHARACTER:

1. A grandparent with character will love his children.
2. A grandparent with character will stay active so that he may continue to serve his family.
3. A grandparent with character will be cautious not to criticize his children's rearing of their children, but help when asked.

CHARACTER

4. A grandparent with character will not become consumed with his old age, but will be consumed with the needs of those who have youth.
5. A grandparent with character will uphold his children's requests and standards while watching the grandchildren.
6. A grandparent with character will consider the requests of the parents concerning their children.
7. A grandparent with character will not cause division between his children and his children's in-laws.
8. A grandparent with character will tell the truth to his grandchildren.
9. A grandparent with character will pass on to his grandchildren good ethics.
10. A grandparent with character will leave a good name for his grandchildren.

Note: After reading this material, a grandparent with character will spend more time developing his own character than he will pointing out the character flaws of others.

THE ATTRIBUTES OF A **STUDENT** WHO POSSESSES CHARACTER:

1. A student with character will be on time to class.
2. A student with character will take note of more than what is the minimum requirement.
3. A student with character will attempt to get an "A" on every test.
4. A student with character will not study just to achieve an "A," but he will study to achieve an education.
5. A student with character will show appreciation for the teacher.
6. A student with character will show admiration for the teacher.
7. A student with character will encourage the teacher by listening.
8. A student with character will not sleep in class.
9. A student with character finishes all of his work.

CHARACTER AND PEOPLE WITH CHARACTER

10. A student with character turns in all of his work on time.
11. A student with character will do extra work — whether or not his grade needs it.
12. A student with character gets the character of the teacher and not just the material the teacher is teaching.
13. A student with character shares with others what he has learned.
14. A student with character never cheats on tests.
15. A student with character never misses class without a good reason.

Note: *After reading this material, a student with character will spend more time developing his own character than he will pointing out the character flaws of others.*

THE ATTRIBUTES OF A **TEACHER** WHO POSSESSES CHARACTER:

1. A teacher with character comes to class prepared.
2. A teacher with character comes to class on time.
3. A teacher with character realizes that he is not only transferring knowledge, but he is also transferring a personality.
4. A teacher with character understands why he is the teacher and why students are students; therefore, he does not treat the students as if they are stupid, but helps them because they are not formally educated.
5. A teacher with character will not allow his expectations to exceed his ability to teach.
6. A teacher with character understands that if his students are failing, he is failing also.
7. A teacher with character makes sure that he has actually transferred knowledge to the student.
8. A teacher with character is always learning.
9. A teacher with character will understand some students sleep because the teacher "rocked" them to sleep.

CHARACTER

10. A teacher with character will teach with enthusiasm.
11. A teacher with character will not teach the same old thing the same old way.
12. A teacher with character should not be forced to demand the students' attention, but he should attempt to try to earn their attention.
13. A teacher with character will learn with the student.
14. A teacher with character teaches in and out of the classroom.
15. A teacher with character fears each student's failure as much as he fears his own failure.

Note: After reading this material, a teacher with character will spend more time developing his own character than he will pointing out the character flaws of others.

THE ATTRIBUTES OF A **POLITICIAN** WHO POSSESSES CHARACTER:

1. A politician with character will keep his promises.
2. A politician with character will think before he talks.
3. A politician with character will realize that if he cannot live by proper morals, standards, and promises, then he should resign his office.
4. A politician with character will always do what is right and not what is convenient.
5. A politician with character is concerned for all whom he represents, not just those with money.
6. A politician with character remembers who placed him in office.
7. A politician with character will keep in touch with the needs of the people and not just his investors.
8. A politician with character understands that that which is ethical to another politician may not be ethical to God.
9. A politician with character remembers that while he is in office he may need a job from a constituent someday.

10. A politician with character is virtually unheard-of.

Note: *After reading this material, a politician with character will spend more time developing his own character than he will pointing out the character flaws of others.*

THE ATTRIBUTES OF A **COACH** WHO POSSESSES CHARACTER:

1. A coach with character will be honest.
2. A coach with character is not concerned with his personal victory of winning a game but with the personal victories of each individual team player.
3. A coach with character is more concerned with character than talent.
4. A coach with character realizes the importance of teamwork.
5. A coach with character takes the time to train his team members to be what they need to be — not what he wants them to be.
6. A coach with character should realize that he is a prominent role model in a youth's life.
7. A coach with character should be morally clean.
8. A coach with character will remember that he coaches on and off the court.
9. A coach with character remembers that life is not just a game.
10. A coach with character believes that winning is not everything.

Note: *After reading this material, a coach with character will spend more time developing his own character than he will pointing out the character flaws of others.*

THE ATTRIBUTES OF A **LENDER** WHO POSSESSES CHARACTER:

1. A lender with character will have patience.

CHARACTER

2. A lender with character will not lend money beyond the borrower's character to repay.
3. A lender with character will not charge ridiculous interest rates.
4. A lender with character will treat others the way he would want to be treated.
5. A lender with character will not drain someone of his life for his own personal glory and success.

Note: *After reading this material, a lender with character will spend more time developing his own character than he will pointing out the character flaws of others.*

THE ATTRIBUTES OF A **BORROWER** WHO POSSESSES CHARACTER:

1. A borrower with character will think before he borrows.
2. A borrower with character will determine that his desire is to borrow only when necessary.
3. A borrower with character will remember that when he is late with a payment, he defrauds the name of the lender. The lender has bills to pay on time as well.
4. The character of a borrower says, "I will pay the full payment on time."
5. The character of a borrower says, "I will someday lend."
6. The character of a borrower says, "If an emergency arises and I cannot pay on time, I will contact in person the lender to alert him of this fact."
7. The character of a borrower says, "I'll pay my loan off early if I can."
8. The character of a borrower says, "I will repay my parents."
9. The character of a borrower says, "I'll return the merchandise in the same condition or better than it was when I received it."
10. The character of a borrower says, "All my financial decisions must not hurt my lender."

CHARACTER AND PEOPLE WITH CHARACTER

Note: After reading this material, the borrower with character will spend more time developing his own character than he will pointing out the character flaws of others.

THE ATTRIBUTES OF AN **AMERICAN** WHO POSSESSES CHARACTER:

1. The character of an American says, "I love my country."
2. The character of an American says, "I will not cheat my country."
3. The character of an American says, "I will not be a draft dodger. If I am a draft dodger, I will not run for President."
4. The character of an American says, "I will stand for the singing or playing of 'The Star-Spangled Banner.' "
5. The character of an American says, "I will place my hand over my heart when I say the Pledge of Allegiance."
6. The character of an American says, "I prefer to buy American-made products."
7. The character of an American says, "While producing American-made products, I will remember that my productivity is a reflection of my nation."
8. The character of an American says, "This is one nation under God, and I should remember Him."
9. The character of an American says, "I will develop my own personal character to strengthen the character and the moral fiber of my country."
10. The character of an American says, "I will vote."

Note: After reading this material, an American with character will spend more time developing his own character than he will pointing out the character flaws of others.

CHARACTER

THE ATTRIBUTES OF A **PREACHER** WHO POSSESSES CHARACTER:

1. The character of a preacher says, "I will preach the truth, no matter what the outcome."
2. The character of a preacher says, "I will live the truth, no matter what the outcome."
3. The character of a preacher says, "I will love my own wife and leave everyone else's alone."
4. The character of a preacher says, "Money will not make decisions for me."
5. The character of a preacher says, "I will be faithful to God."
6. The character of a preacher says, "I will not use my people."
7. The character of a preacher says, "I will not make merchandise of a church."
8. The character of a preacher says, "I will work hard."
9. The character of a preacher says, "I will be fresh and exciting in my preaching."
10. The character of a preacher says, "I will teach others character."
11. The character of a preacher says, "I will feel guilty as the result of giving a poor 30-minute speech to a crowd of 500 people." He has wasted only 30 minutes of his own time, but 250 hours of his congregation's time were wasted.
12. The character of a preacher says, "I have a solution or will seek a solution for every problem." A preacher without character will find a problem for every solution.
13. The character of a preacher says, "I realize there is no such thing as an interesting subject of study. There is only a person who has the character to be interested in study."
14. The character of a preacher says, "I would rather increase my character level to live on $10,000.00 a year less than to have the $10,000.00 increase in pay."
15. The character of a preacher says, "I will spend more time building the character of my people than in building a name for myself."

Note: After reading this material, a preacher with character will spend more time developing his own character than he will pointing out the character flaws of others.

THE ATTRIBUTES OF A **DATING COUPLE** WHO POSSESS CHARACTER:

1. The character of the dating couple says, "We will not date alone, but with chaperons."
2. The character of the dating couple says, "We will not tempt one another."
3. The character of the dating couple says, "We will wait until after marriage to experience the physical benefits of marriage."
4. The character of the dating couple says, "I will treat my date the way I want my own daughter or my own son treated by someone someday."
5. The character of the dating couple is always concerned about their parents' wishes.
6. The character of a young man dating should always be that he would never give a girl a gift expecting something that is improper in exchange.
7. The character of a young girl dating should be that she would never do anything to entice a man into sin.
8. The character of a dating couple says, "My own personal enjoyment is not my only desire; pleasing my God and my parents is also important."
9. The character of a dating couple says, "We will stay moral and clean; when we go to the wedding altar, we will both be pure."
10. The character of a dating couple remembers that they too, one day, may have children of their own whom the parents will want to behave on their dates when the children start dating; therefore, they must live as good examples.
11. The character of a dating couple is never to go to a dark place alone.

CHARACTER

12. The character of a dating couple is never to neck and pet, which leads to immorality.
13. The character of the dating couple is never to talk suggestively.
14. The character of a dating couple would never allow them to hide things from their parents.
15. The character of a dating couple plans a date rather than lets things happen as they will.

Note: After reading this material, a dating couple with character will spend more time developing their own character than pointing out the character flaws of others.

THE ATTRIBUTES OF A **SHOPPER** WHO POSSESSES CHARACTER:

1. The character of a shopper insists that he go to a grocery store with a list which he follows.
2. The character of a shopper is never to spend more than he has.
3. The character of a shopper is to study the product carefully before purchasing it.
4. The character of a shopper is to buy what is nutritious.
5. The character of a shopper is not to purchase a product because of a flashy label.
6. The character of a shopper is not to purchase a product just because of television advertisements and promises.
7. The character of a shopper says, "I may need to sleep on this decision before purchasing."
8. The character of a shopper does not have the desire to please an uncontrolled appetite for the day, thereby forgetting about the rest of the week and, hence, his future.
9. The character of a shopper says, "Do not go grocery shopping when hungry."
10. The character of a shopper is cautious of spring fever when shopping.

CHARACTER AND PEOPLE WITH CHARACTER

Note: After reading this material, a shopper with character will spend more time developing his own character than he will pointing out the character flaws of others.

THE ATTRIBUTES OF A **SALESMAN** WHO POSSESSES CHARACTER:

1. A salesman with character will not sell a product that is not worth selling.
2. A salesman with character will not hurt the buyer.
3. A salesman with character will not oversell a product.
4. A salesman with character owns one of the products which he is selling.
5. A salesman with character is just with his price.
6. A salesman with character stands behind his promises.
7. A salesman with character tells the truth.
8. A salesman with character usually provides a warranty.
9. A salesman with character lives in the same town in which he is selling his product.
10. A salesman with character is willing to give out his home phone number if necessary.
11. A salesman with character returns his customers' calls.
12. A salesman with character would be willing to sell his product to his own mother, father, or preacher.
13. A salesman with character works for a company with character.
14. A salesman with a good reputation will work for a company with a good reputation.
15. A salesman with character can smile when he is not making a sale, as well as when he is trying to make a sale.

Note: After reading this material, a salesman with character will spend more time developing his own character than he will pointing out the character flaws of others.

Chapter 4

Character and Our Employment

A FEW MONTHS AGO, I was invited by a steel company to preach to the men at their dinner break. This chapter is a result of the preaching service at that factory. Any person, saved or unsaved, knows you must have and practice good character if you are going to keep from being fired. Allow me to share some principles that I have learned about being a good employee.

1. Get up, and you will stay employed. Proverbs 6:9 says, *"How long wilt thou sleep, O sluggard? when wilt thou arise out of thy sleep?"* In this verse, God is saying that you need to learn to **get up!** If you do not arise when it is time, you are forming some habits in your life that will eventually destroy you. You may think, "Well, it's just a problem that I have right now. I can and will someday change." No! It's a character problem, and someone cannot wave a magic wand over your head to cure that problem. You must learn to get out of bed in the morning and **get to work.**

Perhaps you think that sleeping late is a stage of life. No, it is a stage when you have poor character. When the alarm goes off in the morning, wake up and get out of bed. There is no conceivable way to get to work if you do not get up! Sleep habits will be discussed in further detail in Chapter 6.

In chapter 1 of the book of Jonah, we find Jonah running from the Lord. His flight takes him to the bottom of a ship. A **lost businessman** (the shipmaster) finds Jonah while he is asleep in the

CHARACTER

bottom of that ship and says, *"O sleeper."* (Jonah 1:6) Why in the world is a **lost businessman** telling a **preacher** to get up? An unsaved businessman should not outwork any Christian! Get up!

2. Show up, and you will stay employed. Ecclesiastes 3:17b says, *"For there is a time there for every purpose and for every work."* Everyone knows you can't **show up** unless you **get up.** Then, you are supposed to show up on time — not fifteen minutes late, not five minutes late, in fact, not even five seconds late. If it takes 25 minutes to drive to work, you don't leave 26 minutes before you have to punch your time clock. You leave **early**. Did it ever occur to you that something could happen? You just might catch one of those red lights that you usually don't catch; you would be late for work! There was a time when people had the character to show up for work or appointments on time.

While I was in college, I worked in Valparaiso, Indiana. When I left for work, I always planned to leave plenty early because I never wanted to be late. I worked in Valparaiso for almost five years, and I was late one time in five years. Let me share with you my one instance of being late. One day after leaving for work, I had a flat tire. When I looked in the trunk of my car, I found the jack handle was gone. I ran **four miles** to the nearest dealership, where I bought a jack handle, ran back to my car, and changed the flat. I arrived at work **one minute** late. Why did I run? Because I was supposed to **show up on time!** I believe the reason why many people are late for work is because they don't care.

Could one of your children get a job today at the place where you work based on your record of attendance and promptness? Many people cannot keep a steady job today because they do not have any character. You might ask, "How did you acquire such a good record?" Quite simply — I planned not to be late. Show up on time, and your employer will give you a steady job.

3. Hurry up, and you will stay employed. Colossians 3:23 says, *"And whatsoever ye do, do it heartily, as to the Lord, and not unto men."* No unsaved person should outwork a Christian. It doesn't matter what you are doing — you are to work hard. Hurry up while you are working. It ought to be said that you are the hardest working

CHARACTER AND OUR EMPLOYMENT

person in that shop.

Allow me to share a personal illustration. I worked as a machinist for ten years, and I don't regret a moment of the time I worked in a machine shop. I wouldn't trade the experience for anything in the world. My foreman thought he would try to provoke me one day, so he came to where I was running a lathe and said, "Jeff, I want you to run two lathes."

"Sure, that would be great!"

"It would?"

I answered, "Yes, I'd be glad to do it!" So I started running two machines. As I was working with the two lathes, I thought, "Why can't I try three?" So, when the boss wasn't watching, I started another machine which was sitting idle. I soon got the knack of how to operate the machine and keep my two lathes running simultaneously, so I started another — a sanding machine to deburr parts.

My boss came over later and said, "What are you doing?!"

"I'm running these four machines!"

"Why?"

I answered, "I thought you wanted me to hurry up."

He said, "What are the other guys going to think?"

I said, "We're not going to need the other guys for long!"

He said, "Excellent!"

Whatever it is you do, be the biggest producer you can be. If you are flipping hamburgers, you ought to flip all you can! If you are moving boxes, you ought to move them faster and better than anybody else. If you are fabricating parts, you ought to outproduce everybody! If you are pushing a broom, you ought to sweep more floors than anyone else, and your floors ought to be the cleanest. If you are a typist, you should type as many words as humanly possible, and you ought to practice in your spare time to increase your speed.

4. Shut up, and you will stay employed. Proverbs 14:23 says, *"In all labour there is profit: but the talk of the lips tendeth only to penury."* This verse quite simply means you need to shut up. Some workers need to stop talking so much at work. The boss shouldn't have to come to you all the time and tell you to work instead of talk.

CHARACTER

Some workers talk too much, and that is why they don't produce more. I can tell you what kind of Christian you are by what your co-workers think of you.

"Shut up" means not to talk negatively about how much you earn. When you accepted the employment, you agreed to work for five dollars an hour. So be quiet, and earn your paycheck.

"Shut up" when you are receiving a scolding — listen and make no defense or argument. If you were right and the boss had misunderstood, keep quiet anyway. You need not go around talking about what you don't like. Don't be a complainer. The Bible has much to say about those who murmured. In Numbers 14, God forbade the children of Israel to enter into the Promised Land because of their murmuring — their complaining, if you please. In I Corinthians 10:10 the Bible says, *"Neither murmur ye, as some of them also murmured, and were destroyed of the destroyer."* Just learn to say two words to yourself that you ought never to say to another — "shut up!"

5. Grow up, and you will stay employed. I Corinthians 13:11 says, *"When I was a child, I spake as a child, I understood as a child, I thought as a child: but when I became a man, I put away childish things."* If you are old enough to seek employment, you are not a child anymore! You no longer cling to mama's apron strings. Grow up!

Part of growing up is ending the practical jokes and pranks at work. That kind of behavior will get you into trouble. You say, "Well, I was just having a little bit of fun." It may have been a little bit of fun for you, but was it fun for the person upon whom you played the prank? When fun is had at the expense of another, someone is always hurt. Have your fun on your own time; work on the boss' time! Your employer cannot afford to pay you to have fun.

When you do not work your work hours, you hurt the name of Christ. You are supposed to work hard because it is right to work hard. *"Whatsoever thy hand findeth to do, do it with thy might."* (Ecclesiastes 9:10a) That verse is a direct command from God.

In order to work, take your hands out of your pockets. My dad used to tell me, "Son, watch out for people who have their hands in their pockets all the time. It's a sign of a lazy person." Most of you who keep your hands in your pockets all the time also have your hands in your boss' pocketbook because you play rather than work.

If there is anything America needs, it is a country full of grown-up, hardworking people who work for every penny they receive. Unfortunately, we have a welfare society with many lazy recipients stealing the money of hardworking people. We have others who take money out of the boss' pockets as they play at work while the diligent workers "bring home the bacon." Are they any different than the welfare seekers? Grow up!

6. Push up, and you will stay employed. Exodus 17:12 says, *"But Moses' hands were heavy; and they took a stone, and put it under him, and he sat thereon; and Aaron and Hur stayed up his hands, the one on the one side, and the other on the other side; and his hands were steady until the going down of the sun."* God's people were battling with the Amalekites. When Moses' hands were uplifted, God's people prevailed. However, when Moses wearied and could no longer lift his hands, the Amalekites prevailed. Two men came to the aid of Moses. They stood beside Moses and helped to hold up his arms, and the Bible says, *"And Joshua discomfited Amalek and his people with the edge of the sword."* (Exodus 17:13) Aaron and Hur helped to sustain Moses by pushing up his hands.

Our society teaches, "Every man for himself." However, the Bible teaches the follower to push up the leader. The owner of a company where I once worked said, "Jeff, you are doing a wonderful job! Some of the things that you have developed here are going very well."

I replied, "Well, my supervisor taught me well. He gave me the opportunity." Shortly thereafter, the owner called my supervisor into his office and gave **him** a raise.

"What did you do, Brother Owens? Did you get angry? You deserved the raise instead of the supervisor." It wasn't my place to question his raise. It was my place to "push up" my supervisor. By the way, when review day came, my supervisor said to me, "You deserve a raise."

I received almost every one of my raises because I gave some credit to somebody else who deserved part of it. Give your boss some credit! You ought to treat your boss the same way you would want to be treated if you were the boss. The problem is that many of you don't have the character to get where he is so you want to pull him down to where you are.

7. Move up is what you will do. Proverbs 12:24 teaches, *"The hand of the diligent shall bear rule: but the slothful shall be under tribute."* When you are busy pushing up and lifting your employer, the company is moving up. You are going to move up with the company if you will follow these simple principles. The American way seems to be to cut someone else's throat in order to move up. Unfortunately, those who move up in that way will never receive the trust of those in the ranks. The Christian way is to build your boss and forget yourself. Ask yourself these questions: "If your boss went to the top today, would he want you there alongside him? Would he trust you?" America is dying for some people of character who are hard-working and honest. No employer wants disloyal, back-stabbing employees.

By using these seven two-word principles, you will excel in the workplace. You will receive the praise and recommendation of co-workers, supervisors, and employers. Be a person of great character at your place of employment. Remember, your work ethic reflects your God.

Character and Our Employment

1. **Get Up!** *"How long wilt thou sleep, O sluggard? when wilt thou arise out of thy sleep?"* (Proverbs 6:9)

2. **Show Up!** *"For there is a time there for every purpose and for every work."* (Ecclesiastes 3:17b)

3. **Hurry Up!** *"And whatsoever ye do, do it heartily, as to the Lord, and not unto men."* (Colossians 3:23)

4. **Shut Up!** *"In all labour there is profit: but the talk of the lips tendeth only to penury."* (Proverbs 14:23)

5. **Grow Up!** *"When I was a child, I spake as a child, I understood as a child, I thought as a child: but when I became a man, I put away childish things."* (I Corinthians 13:11)

6. **Push Up!** *"But Moses' hands were heavy; and they took a stone, and put it under him, and he sat thereon; and Aaron and Hur stayed up his hands, the one on the one side, and the other on the other side; and his hands were steady until the going down of the sun."* (Exodus 17:12)

The result is, you will . . .

7. **Move Up!** *"The hand of the diligent shall bear rule: but the slothful shall be under tribute."* (Proverbs 12:24)

– Dr. Jeff Owens

Chapter 5

Character and the Bible, a Book Full of Good Workers

AS WE START IN the book of Genesis and read through all 66 books of the Bible and end up in the book of Revelation, we find job description after job description. Our God is a God Who believes that man should work. God placed man in the Garden of Eden to work, and from that day until this God has expected man to work. A Biblical character trait missing from our day is hard work. The following is a list of workers found in the Bible.

Old Testament Workers and Job Descriptions

Fruit Gatherer
"And in process of time it came to pass, that Cain brought of the fruit of the ground an offering unto the LORD." (Genesis 4:3)

Husbandman
"And Noah began to be an husbandman." (Genesis 9:20a)

Brickmaker
"And they said one to another, Go to, let us make brick, and burn them throughly." (Genesis 11:3a)

Binder of Sheaves
"For, behold, we were binding sheaves in the field." (Genesis 37:7a)

CHARACTER

Butler
> *"And it came to pass after these things, that the butler ...."*
> (Genesis 40:1)

Guard
> *"And the captain of the guard charged Joseph with them."*
> (Genesis 40:4a)

Chief Butler
> *"And the chief butler ...."* (Genesis 40:9)

Baker
> *"And it came to pass the third day, which was Pharaoh's birthday, that he made a feast unto all his servants: and he lifted up the head of the chief butler and of the chief baker ...."* (Genesis 40:20)

Midwife
> *"And he said, When ye do the office of a midwife."* (Exodus 1:16a)

Taskmaster
> *"And the LORD said, I have surely seen the affliction of my people which are in Egypt, and have heard their cry by reason of their taskmasters; for I know their sorrows."* (Exodus 3:7)

Cattleman
> *"Send therefore now, and gather thy cattle, and all that thou hast in the field."* (Exodus 9:19a)

Candlestick Maker
> *"And thou shalt make a candlestick of pure gold: of beaten work shall the candlestick be made."* (Exodus 25:31a)

Maker of Lamps
> *"And thou shalt make the seven lamps thereof: and they shall light the lamps thereof, that they may give light over against it."*
> (Exodus 25:37a)

Seamstress
"And thou shalt make holy garments for Aaron thy brother for glory and for beauty." (Exodus 28:2)

Apothecary
"And thou shalt make it an oil of holy ointment, an ointment compound after the art of the apothecary." (Exodus 30:25a)

Furniture Maker
"And I, behold, I have given with him Aholiab, the son of Ahisamach, of the tribe of Dan: and in the hearts of all that are wise hearted I have put wisdom, that they may make all that I have commanded thee." (Exodus 31:6)

Embroiderer
"Them hath he filled with wisdom of heart, to work all manner of work, of the engraver, and of the cunning workman, and of the embroiderer." (Exodus 35:35a)

Engraver
"Them hath he filled with wisdom of heart, to work all manner of work, of the engraver." (Exodus 35:35a)

Footman
"And Moses said, The people, among whom I am, are six hundred thousand footmen." (Numbers 11:21a)

Maidservant
"But the seventh day is the sabbath of the LORD thy God: in it thou shalt not do any work, thou, nor thy son, nor thy daughter, nor thy manservant, nor thy maidservant." (Deuteronomy 5:14a)

Manservant
"Neither shalt thou desire thy neighbour's wife, neither shalt thou covet thy neighbour's house, his field, or his manservant." (Deuteronomy 5:21a)

CHARACTER

Woodworker
"At that time the LORD said unto me, Hew thee two tables of stone like unto the first, and come up unto me into the mount, and make thee an ark of wood." (Deuteronomy 10:1)

Hewer of Wood
"Your little ones, your wives, and thy stranger that is in thy camp, from the hewer of thy wood ...." (Deuteronomy 29:11)

Drawer of Water
"And Joshua made them that day hewers of wood and drawers of water for the congregation." (Joshua 9:27a)

Soothsayer
"Balaam also the son of Beor, the soothsayer." (Joshua 13:22a)

Swordsman
"Now Zebah and Zalmunna were in Karkor, and their hosts with them, about fifteen thousand men, all that were left of all the hosts of the children of the east: for there fell an hundred and twenty thousand men that drew sword." (Judges 8:10)

Armorbearer
"Then he called hastily unto the young man his armourbearer, and said unto him, Draw thy sword." (Judges 9:54a)

Handmaid
"Then she said, Let me find favour in thy sight, my lord; for that thou hast comforted me, and for that thou hast spoken friendly unto thine handmaid ...." (Ruth 2:13)

Nurse
"And Naomi took the child, and laid it in her bosom, and became nurse unto it." (Ruth 4:16)

Chariot Maker
"And he will appoint him captains over thousands, and captains over

CHARACTER AND THE BIBLE, A BOOK FULL OF WORKERS

fifties; and will set them to ear his ground, and to reap his harvest, and to make his instruments of war, and instruments of his chariots." (I Samuel 8:12)

Confectionary
"And he will take your daughters to be confectionaries."
(I Samuel 8:13a)

Cook
"And Samuel said unto the cook, Bring the portion which I gave thee." (I Samuel 9:23a)

Goat Herder
"And there was a man in Maon, whose possessions were in Carmel; and the man was very great, and he had three thousand sheep, and a thousand goats: and he was shearing his sheep in Carmel."
(I Samuel 25:2)

Sheepshearers
"And there was a man in Maon, whose possessions were in Carmel; and the man was very great, and he had three thousand sheep, and a thousand goats: and he was shearing his sheep in Carmel."
(I Samuel 25:2)

Archer
"And the battle went sore against Saul, and the archers ...."
(I Samuel 31:3)

Runner
"Then Adonijah the son of Haggith exalted himself, saying, I will be king: and he prepared him chariots and horsemen, and fifty men to run before him. (I Kings 1:5)

Worker in Brass
"He was a widow's son of the tribe of Naphtali, and his father was a man of Tyre, a worker in brass." (I Kings 7:14a)

CHARACTER

Cupbearer
> "And the meat of his table, and the sitting of his servants, and the attendance of his ministers, and their apparel, and his cupbearers." (I Kings 10:5a)

Spice Merchants
> "Beside that he had of the merchantmen, and of the traffick of the spice merchants." (I Kings 10:15a)

Trench Digger
> "And with the stones he built an altar in the name of the LORD: and he made a trench." (I Kings 18:32a)

Shipbuilder
> "Jehoshaphat made ships ...." (I Kings 22:48)

Sheepmaster
> "And Mesha king of Moab was a sheepmaster, and rendered unto the king of Israel an hundred thousand lambs, and an hundred thousand rams, with the wool." (II Kings 3:4a)

Builder
> "And they gave the money, being told, into the hands of them that did the work, that had the oversight of the house of the LORD: and they laid it out to the carpenters and builders, that wrought upon the house of the LORD." (II Kings 12:11)

Mason
> "Now Hiram king of Tyre sent messengers to David, and timber of cedars, with masons and carpenters, to build him an house." (I Chronicles 14:1)

Overseer
> "And he set threescore and ten thousand of them to be bearers of burdens, and fourscore thousand to be hewers in the mountain, and three thousand and six hundred overseers to set the people a work." (II Chronicles 2:18)

CHARACTER AND THE BIBLE, A BOOK FULL OF WORKERS

Chapman
"Beside that which chapmen and merchants brought."
(II Chronicles 9:14a)

Chariot Driver
"And a certain man drew a bow at a venture, and smote the king of Israel between the joints of the harness: therefore he said to his chariot man, Turn thine hand, that thou mayest carry me out of the host; for I am wounded." (II Chronicles 18:33)

Recorder
"Now in the eighteenth year of his reign, when he had purged the land, and the house, he sent Shaphan the son of Azaliah, and Maaseiah the governor of the city, and Joah the son of Joahaz the recorder, to repair the house of the LORD his God."
(II Chronicles 34:8)

Wardrobe Keeper
"And Hilkiah, and they that the king had appointed, went to Huldah the prophetess, the wife of Shallum, the son of Tikvath, the son of Hasrah, keeper of the wardrobe." (II Chronicles 34:22a)

Carpenter
"They gave money also unto the masons, and to the carpenters."
(Ezra 3:7a)

Chancellor
"Then wrote Rehum the chancellor ...." (Ezra 4:9)

Porter
And there went up some of the children of Israel, and of the priests, and the Levites ... and the porters." (Ezra 7:7)

Lieutenant
"And they delivered the king's commissions unto the king's lieutenants." (Ezra 8:36a)

CHARACTER

A King's Forest Keeper
"And a letter unto Asaph the keeper of the king's forest ...." (Nehemiah 2:8)

Security System Installer
"But the fish gate did the sons of Hassenaah build, who also laid the beams thereof, and set up the doors thereof, the locks thereof, and the bars thereof." (Nehemiah 3:3)

Goldsmith
"Next unto him repaired Uzziel the son of Harhaiah, of the goldsmiths ...." (Nehemiah 3:8)

Furnace Repairman
"Malchijah the son of Harim, and Hashub the son of Pahath-moab, repaired the other piece, and the tower of the furnaces."
(Nehemiah 3:11)

Seller
"So the merchants and sellers of all kind of ware ...."
(Nehemiah 13:20)

New Testament Workers and Job Descriptions

Minstrel
"And when Jesus came into the ruler's house, and saw the minstrels." (Matthew 9:23a)

Reapers
"Let both grow together until the harvest: and in the time of harvest I will say to the reapers, Gather ye together first the tares, and bind them in bundles to burn them: but gather the wheat into my barn." (Matthew 13:30)

Tetrarch
"At that time Herod the tetrarch ...." (Matthew 14:1)

CHARACTER AND THE BIBLE, A BOOK FULL OF WORKERS

Tormentor
> *"And his lord was wroth, and delivered him to the tormentors, till he should pay all that was due unto him."* (Matthew 18:34)

Farmer
> *"But they made light of it, and went their ways, one to his farm, another to his merchandise."* (Matthew 22:5)

Exchanger
> *"Thou oughtest therefore to have put my money to the exchangers."* (Matthew 25:27a)

Physician
> *"When Jesus heard it, he saith unto them, They that are whole have no need of the physician."* (Mark 2:17a)

Swine Herder
> *"And they that fed the swine fled, and told it in the city, and in the country. And they went out to see what it was that was done."* (Mark 5:14)

Executioner
> *"And immediately the king sent an executioner."* (Mark 6:27a)

Fuller
> *"And his raiment became shining, exceeding white as snow; so as no fuller on earth can white them."* (Mark 9:3)

Moneychanger
> *"And they come to Jerusalem: and Jesus went into the temple, and began to cast out them that sold and bought in the temple, and overthrew the tables of the moneychangers ...."* (Mark 11:15)

Fisherman
> *"And saw two ships standing by the lake: but the fishermen were gone out of them, and were washing their nets."* (Luke 5:2)

CHARACTER

Publican
"And after these things he went forth, and saw a publican."
(Luke 5:27a)

Lawyer
"And, behold, a certain lawyer." (Luke 10:25a)

Hotel Manager
"And on the morrow when he departed, he took out two pence, and gave them to the host, and said unto him, Take care of him; and whatsoever thou spendest more, when I come again, I will repay thee." (Luke 10:35)

Officer
"When thou goest with thine adversary to the magistrate, as thou art in the way, give diligence that thou mayest be delivered from him; lest he hale thee to the judge, and the judge deliver thee to the officer, and the officer cast thee into prison." (Luke 12:58)

Sweeper
"Either what woman having ten pieces of silver, if she lose one piece, doth not light a candle, and sweep the house, and seek diligently till she find it?" (Luke 15:8)

Beggar
"And there was a certain beggar ...." (Luke 16:20)

Judge
"Saying, There was in a city a judge, which feared not God, neither regarded man." (Luke 18:2)

Rabbi
"The same came to Jesus by night, and said unto him, Rabbi, we know that thou art a teacher come from God." (John 3:2a)

CHARACTER AND THE BIBLE, A BOOK FULL OF WORKERS

Gardener
"Jesus saith unto her, Woman, why weepest thou? whom seekest thou? She, supposing him to be the gardener ...." (John 20:15)

Apostle
"And they gave forth their lots; and the lot fell upon Matthias; and he was numbered with the eleven apostles." (Acts 1:26)

Queen
"And he arose and went: and, behold, a man of Ethiopia, an eunuch of great authority under Candace queen of the Ethiopians, who had the charge of all her treasure, and had come to Jerusalem for to worship." (Acts 8:27)

Tanner
"He lodgeth with one Simon a tanner, whose house is by the sea side: he shall tell thee what thou oughtest to do." (Acts 10:6)

Soldier
"And when he had apprehended him, he put him in prison, and delivered him to four quaternions of soldiers to keep him."
(Acts 12:4a)

Sergeant
"And the serjeants told these words unto the magistrates ...." (Acts 16:38)

Philosopher
"Then certain philosophers of the Epicureans ...." (Acts 17:18a)

Poet
"For in him we live, and move, and have our being; as certain also of your own poets have said ...." (Acts 17:28)

Tentmaker
"And because he was of the same craft, he abode with them, and

CHARACTER

wrought: for by their occupation they were tentmakers."
(Acts 18:3)

Deputy
"And when Gallio was the deputy of Achaia." (Acts 18:12a)

Silversmith
"For a certain man named Demetrius, a silversmith, which made silver shrines for Diana." (Acts 19:24a)

Town Clerk
"And when the townclerk had appeased the people." (Acts 19:35a)

Evangelist
"And the next day we that were of Paul's company departed, and came unto Cæsarea: and we entered into the house of Philip the evangelist ...." (Acts 21:8)

Centurion
"And he commanded a centurion to keep Paul." (Acts 24:23a)

Shipman
"And as the shipmen were about to flee out of the ship, when they had let down the boat into the sea ...." (Acts 27:30)

Minister
"For for this cause pay ye tribute also: for they are God's ministers ...." (Romans 13:6)

Chamberlain
"Gaius mine host, and of the whole church, saluteth you. Erastus the chamberlain of the city saluteth you ...." (Romans 16:23)

Sower
"Now he that ministereth seed to the sower ...."
(II Corinthians 9:10)

Spy
"And that because of false brethren unawares brought in, who came in privily to spy out our liberty." (Galatians 2:4a)

Schoolmaster
"But after that faith is come, we are no longer under a schoolmaster." (Galatians 3:25)

Tutor
"But is under tutors ...." (Galatians 4:2)

Bishop
"Paul and Timotheus, the servants of Jesus Christ, to all the saints in Christ Jesus which are at Philippi, with the bishops ...." (Philippians 1:1)

Deacon
"Paul and Timotheus, the servants of Jesus Christ, to all the saints in Christ Jesus which are at Philippi, with the bishops and deacons." (Philippians 1:1)

Servant
"Masters, give unto your servants that which is just and equal." (Colossians 4:1a)

Coppersmith
"Alexander the coppersmith ...." (II Timothy 4:14)

Teacher
"The aged women likewise, that they be in behaviour as becometh holiness, not false accusers, not given to much wine, teachers of good things." (Titus 2:3)

Magistrate
"Put them in mind to be subject to principalities and powers, to obey magistrates." (Titus 3:1a)

CHARACTER

Steward
"As every man hath received the gift, even so minister the same one to another, as good stewards ...." (I Peter 4:10)

Preacher
"And spared not the old world, but saved Noah the eighth person, a preacher of righteousness ...." (II Peter 2:5)

Sailor
"For in one hour so great riches is come to nought. And every shipmaster, and all the company in ships, and sailors, and as many as trade by sea, stood afar off." (Revelation 18:17)

Shipmaster
"For in one hour so great riches is come to nought. And every shipmaster ...." (Revelation 18:17)

Harper
"And the voice of harpers ...." (Revelation 18:22)

Our God is a God of work. He blesses hard work. If you wonder what you could do with your time, just choose a job — an honorable job — and go at it!

Note: It is a wise thing for every man to develop a trade. I was a machinist. My father had a trade as well. It was no accident that Luke was a doctor and Noah a shipbuilder. God had His Son Jesus born into the home of a carpenter for a reason. A man should help his son develop a trade.

Chapter 6

Character and Our Sleep Habits

THE PROPER AMOUNT OF sleep is essential for being a good Christian. Most people do what they want concerning how much time they allow for sleep. Too much sleep or the lack of sleep can bring many undesirable consequences. Allow me to share how sleep affected the lives of some well-known individuals in the Bible.

1. A Christian must not foolishly starve his body of sleep. In I Kings 18:18-40 the story of Elijah defeating the false prophets of Baal on Mt. Carmel is chronicled. Elijah issues a challenge to the false prophets of Baal concerning their god and the one true God. As a result, the false prophets decided to have a showdown to find out whose God was almighty and omnipotent.

Elijah tells the false prophets to offer a sacrifice, call on the name of their god, and let the god answer by fire. The Bible says in verse 26, *"And they took the bullock which was given them, and they dressed it, and called on the name of Baal from morning even until noon, saying, O Baal, hear us. But there was no voice, nor any that answered...."* Even leaping upon their altar and cutting themselves with knives and lancets until they were bloody failed to bring the desired results.

The Bible says in verse 27 that *"Elijah mocked them, and said, Cry aloud: for he is a god; either he is talking, or he is pursuing, or he is in a journey, or peradventure he sleepeth, and must be awaked."* In essence Elijah was saying their god was sleeping or had gone on

CHARACTER

vacation and couldn't hear them! Finally, Elijah repairs the broken-down altar of the Lord, makes a trench around the altar, places the wood on the altar, and cuts the bullock in pieces in preparation for God's fire. However, Elijah wants to be sure the people see the power of the real God. In verse 33 Elijah says, *"Fill four barrels with water, and pour it on the burnt-sacrifice, and on the wood."* Barrels of water were filled not once, but three times! *"And the water ran round about the altar; and he filled the trench also with water."* (I Kings 18:35)

Of course, God heard Elijah's prayer. *"Then the fire of the LORD fell, and consumed the burnt-sacrifice, and the wood, and the stones, and the dust, and licked up the water that was in the trench."* (I Kings 18:38)

Four hundred and fifty false prophets of Baal were present. They heard Elijah pray and ask God to send the fire from Heaven. The Bible says that Elijah then slaughtered the 450 false prophets of Baal that day — one man slaughtered 450 false prophets!

After Elijah had finished defeating the prophets of Baal, Jezebel, who the Bible says *"stirred up"* Ahab (her husband) *"to work wickedness in the sight of the LORD"* (I Kings 21:25), heard of his powerful demonstration. No doubt Queen Jezebel had attended the church of the now-dead false prophets. She sent a messenger to Elijah saying, *"So let the gods do to me, and more also, if I make not thy life as the life of one of them by to morrow about this time."* (I Kings 19:2) In other words, Jezebel pronounced the death sentence for Elijah. Remember, Elijah had just fought and defeated 450 false prophets; now Jezebel is attacking him. Elijah flees for his life.

I have heard preachers say, "What kind of a man would run from a woman?" I contend a real man who had just killed 450 false prophets would run from her because he was tired and worn out.

Not only was Elijah physically exhausted from the battle on Mt. Carmel, he also ran a footrace! Elijah ran from Mt. Carmel to Jezreel (somewhere between 40-60 miles away), and he arrived at the gates of the city before Ahab, who was traveling in his chariot! *"And the hand of the LORD was on Elijah; and he girded up his loins, and ran before Ahab to the entrance of Jezreel."* (I Kings 18:46)

No doubt Elijah was anxious and fatigued when he dejectedly sat

CHARACTER AND OUR SLEEP HABITS

under the juniper tree and cried out, *"It is enough; now, O LORD, take away my life; for I am not better than my fathers."* (I Kings 19:4) I believe God did something special for Elijah at that moment; I believe he gave him peaceful sleep. When it was time for Elijah to awaken, God sent an angel to touch him. Not only did God provide his prophet with peaceful sleep, he had food and water prepared. God knew exactly how long Elijah had been without rest. He also knew exactly how much sleep Elijah needed to replenish his body.

2. A Christian must not be perceived as a "sleeper" by unsaved people. Jonah 1:6b says, *"What meanest thou, O sleeper?"* God had commanded Jonah to go to Nineveh and preach to the people. However, Jonah did not want to go to Nineveh. Instead, he paid fare to go on a ship to Tarshish. The Bible says that while Jonah was running from God he went to the bottom of the ship and went to sleep. While Jonah was sleeping, a storm blew in that threatened the safety of the ship. The mariners were afraid and began to lighten the ship, and the people cried out to their individual gods. In Jonah 1:6 the Bible says that a heathen (probably lost) businessman went to the sleeping Jonah and said, *"What meanest thou, O sleeper? arise, call upon thy God, if so be that God will think upon us, that we perish not."* Are you, like Jonah, a sleeper?

3. A Christian must not sleep to avoid conviction. Jesus slept within God's will; however, Jonah slept as a way of disregarding God's will for him to go to Nineveh. I believe Jonah wanted to sleep so he wouldn't think about what he should have been doing. No doubt Jonah had to get to sleep because he wasn't obeying God. Are you like Jonah? Are you sleeping in order to avoid some responsibility given to you by God?

4. A Christian ought not to sleep while others go to battle. *"And it came to pass in an eveningtide, that David arose from off his bed, and walked upon the roof of the king's house: and from the roof he saw a woman washing herself; and the woman was very beautiful to look upon."* (II Samuel 11:2) The Bible says at *"eveningtide"* — in other words, David had slept all day long! When David decided to sleep in that day, he slept too long. While the armies were out to battle, the commander in chief was resting and idle. During this time of idleness, David saw a woman bathing, lusted after her, committed adultery with her, and, in order to cover the sin, had her husband killed.

I believe that a person ought to work hard because it will help keep him pure. Every young lady ought to work hard because it will help keep her pure. Every young man ought to work hard because it will help keep him pure. If a young man or a young lady works hard enough, by the end of the day they won't want to go out and be immoral. However, they will want to rest!

5. A Christian ought to flee from spiritual defeat rather than sleep. In Judges 13-16, the Bible records the downfall of a man about whom it was said that *"the Spirit of the LORD came upon him"* more than any other man in the Bible.

Delilah holds Samson captive to her demands and whims. She begs, cries, and pleads to know the secret of his strength. Each time Samson tells her the "secret," she immediately calls Philistine cohorts to carry out his answer. Each consecutive answer leads her closer to the truth, when finally he answers truthfully and shows her his heart. *"And she made him sleep upon her knees; and she called for a man, and she caused him to shave off the seven locks of his head; and she began to afflict him, and his strength went from him."* (Judges 16:19)

Mighty Samson takes a nap at the request of a deceitful woman, and when he awakens, he does not know he has lost all of his power! *"And she said, The Philistines be upon thee, Samson. And he awoke out of his sleep, and said, I will go out as at other times before, and shake myself. And he wist not that the LORD was departed from him."* (Judges 16:20) The worst thing about this loss of power is that Samson **knew** she was trying to get his spiritual power, but he took his nap anyway. Samson slept instead of fleeing from spiritual defeat.

6. A Christian ought not to sleep when he should be praying. The Bible says in Matthew 26 that it was time for a great spiritual battle. Jesus was about to go to the cross. In Matthew 26:34 Jesus foretells Peter's denial. *"Jesus said unto him, Verily I say unto thee, That this night, before the cock crow, thou shalt deny me thrice."* Peter answers, *"Though I should die with thee, yet will I not deny thee."* (Matthew 26:35a)

CHARACTER AND OUR SLEEP HABITS

Peter, James, and John then went with Jesus to the Garden of Gethsemane where Jesus said, *"Sit ye here, while I go and pray yonder."* (Matthew 26:36b) When Jesus returns from praying, He finds the three asleep! Once again Jesus charges them to pray. *"Watch and pray, that ye enter not into temptation: the spirit indeed is willing, but the flesh is weak."* (Matthew 26:41) Upon His return, He finds them sleeping again. This time He leaves without awakening them. Jesus returns a third time to find the disciples still sleeping. Probably in resignation He says, *"Sleep on now, and take your rest."* (Matthew 26:45b)

The disciples were supposed to be praying before the battle. That is exactly what every Christian has to do. However, many Christians are just like Peter, James, and John. When the battles come, it is easier to sleep than face it. A Christian can be facing a serious battle, but instead of praying, he is sleeping!

The Bible says that after Jesus was taken by the chief priests and soldiers, Peter followed from a distance. *"But Peter followed him afar off unto the high priest's palace, and went in, and sat with the servants, to see the end."* (Matthew 26:58) As Peter stood at the door, a damsel asked him if he were one of the disciples. Peter answered, *"I am not."* (John 18:17) The Bible says it was cold, so the servants and officers built a fire. Peter stood with them and warmed himself at their fire.

"And when he was gone out into the porch, another maid saw him, and said unto them that were there, This fellow was also with Jesus of Nazareth. And again he denied with an oath, I do not know the man." (Matthew 26:71, 72) Once again Peter is told that he was a disciple because his speech betrayed him, and Peter *"... began ... to curse and to swear, saying, I know not the man. And immediately the cock crew."* (Matthew 26:74)

When Jesus told Peter he would deny his Lord, Jesus didn't mention that Peter would curse and swear and lie. Why did Peter first deny Christ, then lie about knowing Him and curse and swear? I believe it may be because he fell asleep three times instead of praying as Jesus bid him to do. Perhaps he committed one sin for each time he fell asleep when he should have been praying. Don't be like Peter

CHARACTER

and sleep instead of pray.

7. A Christian who sleeps in church and does not listen to the man of God may someday pay with his life. Acts 20:9 says, *"And there sat in a window a certain young man named Eutychus, being fallen into a deep sleep: and as Paul was long preaching, he sunk down with sleep, and fell down from the third loft, and was taken up dead."* This young man slept during the preaching, and he fell from a balcony and died.

You say, "That doesn't happen in today's churches! There are safety features that would prevent a fall." That may very well be true. However, the Bible promises that the length of life will be shortened for the person who does not listen to the man of God preach the Word of God. *"My son, attend to my words; incline thine ear unto my sayings. Let them not depart from thine eyes; keep them in the midst of thine heart. For they are life unto those that find them, and health to all their flesh."* (Proverbs 4:20-22) Sit up in church; it will keep you awake! I believe it is sinful to sleep during the preaching.

8. You will not sleep well when you have made unwise decisions. In Daniel 6:18, the Bible says, *"Then the king went to his palace, and passed the night fasting: neither were instruments of musick brought before him: and his sleep went from him."* The king spoken of in this passage was Darius. He had signed a decree that whoever asked anything of any God or any person for 30 days except of the king would be thrown into a den of lions. When the king hastily signed this decree, he did not realize how adversely it would affect someone he loved. Of course, Daniel was thrown in the lions' den for praying to the true God. King Darius could not sleep knowing what harm his signature had caused. A guilty conscience will rob you of sleep.

Allow me to share some Biblical principles about the matter of sleep.

1. The best way in the world to sleep is God's way. Proverbs 3:19-24 says, *"The LORD by wisdom hath founded the earth; by understanding hath he established the heavens. By his knowledge the depths are broken up, and the clouds drop down the dew. My son, let*

CHARACTER AND OUR SLEEP HABITS

not them depart from thine eyes: keep sound wisdom and discretion: So shall they be life unto thy soul, and grace to thy neck. Then shalt thou walk in thy way safely, and thy foot shall not stumble. When thou liest down, thou shalt not be afraid: ***yea, thou shalt lie down, and thy sleep shall be sweet.***" Sleeping using the wisdom of God means sleeping according to Bible principles.

2. Excess sleep is a thief. Proverbs 24:33 and 34 says, *"Yet a little sleep, a little slumber, a little folding of the hands to sleep: So shall thy poverty come as one that travelleth; and thy want as an armed man."* Someone has said that lost time is never found again. When a person wastes too much time sleeping, that time is never made up.

Consider the phrase, *"and thy want as an armed man."* I believe this means that a lover of sleep has let a robber into his life! That robber is the armed man of sleep, and he is stealing your life from you.

Stop and think of the times that you have missed important events because you were sleeping. Did you miss your soul-winning club? Who might not be in Heaven today because you loved your sleep? Think of all the people who do not attend church every Sunday because they need that extra sleep.

3. Get up immediately when the alarm goes off. Proverbs 6:10 and 11 says, *"Yet a little sleep, a little slumber, a little folding of the hands to sleep: So shall thy poverty come as one that travelleth, and thy want as an armed man."* When God repeats a verse word for word, I believe He really wants us to take note of that idea.

In today's vernacular, this verse means that you ought to break the snooze button on your alarm clock! When the alarm goes off, get up the first time the alarm rings. If a hard worker has become lazy, it is probably because he started getting a little "extra" rest. He probably stopped working extra and started taking a little extra rest.

4. Be cautious of sleeping too much. Proverbs 19:15 says, *"Slothfulness casteth into a deep sleep; and an idle soul shall suffer hunger."* I believe that sleeping too much causes a person to crave even more sleep. If you sleep too much when you do get up, you will still feel tired. You wonder, "Why do I need so much sleep?" The

CHARACTER

answer is quite simple — you are lazy, and you sleep too much! Too much sleep will disable you and steal your strength.

5. Do not be a lover of sleep. Proverbs 20:13a says, *"Love not sleep, lest thou come to poverty."* People put a lot of time and energy into the activities and things they love. Into what do you put the most time? Do you love God more than you love sleep? Do you love sleep more than success?

6. Hard workers who sleep God's way enjoy their food. Proverbs 20:13 says, *"Love not sleep, lest thou come to poverty; open thine eyes, and thou shalt be satisfied with bread."* The Bible says that the man who is a hard worker and earns his money will enjoy his bread. I can tell you something about lazy folks who like to sleep all the time — they can never acquire enough! Their food does not satisfy! Their television gets boring!

After I have put in a good, hard day of work, I will eat just about anything and enjoy it. Some of the most miserable people I know are on welfare and food stamps. They sleep all the time, and they do not enjoy the food a hardworking man puts in their lazy stomachs.

7. Too much sleep will bring poverty. Proverbs 6:10 and 11 says, *"Yet a little sleep, a little slumber, a little folding of the hands to sleep: So shall thy poverty come as one that travelleth, and thy want as an armed man."* Nine out of ten times, a person should work more instead of sleeping longer. Don't be lazy — needing a little extra sleep will bring poverty. If a person sleeps on the job, his boss has a Biblical right to fire him. Not only is sleeping on the job negligent, it is crooked.

8. There is a right time to sleep. Proverbs 10:5 says, *"He that gathereth in summer is a wise son: but he that sleepeth in harvest is a son that causeth shame."* In most cases, a person had better sleep at the conclusion of something and not at its inception. Sleep when the job is done. Once the work is finished, a person will sleep better, and the job will probably get done better.

9. A Christian who cannot get to sleep should pray for God's help. In Psalm 4:1 and 8 the Bible says, *"Hear me when I call, O God ... and hear my prayer. I will both lay me down in peace, and sleep: for thou, LORD, only makest me dwell in safety."* David

CHARACTER AND OUR SLEEP HABITS

realized that the Creator of the universe could put him to sleep in peace. Pray and ask God to make the amount of sleep you are able to get adequate for the work He needs you to do.

In conclusion, let the Bible determine how you sleep. It was in God's plan for all people to sleep during the evening hours. I believe God made darkness because He knew His people needed sleep; therefore, He provided a time for His people to sleep — at night! That means that young people are not supposed to be carousing all night. Often, mothers and fathers cannot understand why their teenage daughter is expecting a child outside the boundaries of marriage. After all, that child is very trustworthy. However, scientists have proven in studies that the mental defenses and inhibitions weaken during the late hours. Children, teenagers, and, yes, even adults ought to be sleeping during the evening hours. It is God's divine plan.

Chapter 7

The Ten Commandments of Character

1.
Thou shalt be on time for everything, every time.

2.
Thou shalt do what is right,
not what is easy or convenient.

3.
Thou shalt work as hard for others
as thou wouldst have them work for thee.

4.
Thou shalt earn the right to own thy property.

5.
Thou shalt respond to the alarm the first time it rings,
and thou shalt arise early in the morning.

6.
Thou shalt finish everything thou hast started.

CHARACTER

7.
Thou shalt record each failure as another way
not to succeed.
Then thou shalt try another way,
and thou shalt never quit until thou hast succeeded.

8.
Thou shalt take no shortcut that will diminish
the quality of thy finished product.

9.
Thou shalt live within the confines of thy means
and not within the confines of thy credit card limits.

10.
Thou shalt control thyself
so that others are not forced to control thee.

Chapter 8

Character and Having a Good Name to Reflect It

THE BIBLE SAYS IN Acts 11:21-26, *"And the hand of the Lord was with them: and a great number believed, and turned unto the Lord. Then tidings of these things came unto the ears of the church which was in Jerusalem: and they sent forth Barnabas, that he should go as far as Antioch. Who, when he came, and had seen the grace of God, was glad, and exhorted them all, that with purpose of heart they would cleave unto the Lord. For he was a good man, and full of the Holy Ghost and of faith: and much people was added unto the Lord. Then departed Barnabas to Tarsus, for to seek Saul: And when he had found him, he brought him unto Antioch. And it came to pass, that a whole year they assembled themselves with the church, and taught much people. And the disciples were called Christians first in Antioch."*

God's people were first called Christians at Antioch. His people behaved so much like Christ that they were associated with Him. The word *Christian* means *Christ-like*. Having the name of "Christian" is an honor and ought to be treated as such. When prospective parents choose a name for the child who will be coming into their home, they spend time reading books which give the origin and meaning of names being considered. Perhaps you have noticed people avoid naming their children Jezebel, Benedict (Arnold), Judas, and Cain. These names are usually not chosen because of a lack of respect for the bearer of the name. Every parent wants his child to have a good name. *"A good name is rather to be chosen than great riches."* (Proverbs 22:1a)

What kind of name do you have? Your name is merely a label on the outside that reflects what you are on the inside. You could have a name like "Joshua," the great military leader in the Bible, and still be a coward. With this introduction in mind, let me share some important truths about having a good name.

1. As Christians, we represent the name of God. II Corinthians 3:2 reminds us, *"Ye are our epistle written in our hearts, known and read of all men."* The Bible says a Christian is like a letter that people read. What do the unsaved "read" in your life? Is your life a condensed version of the Bible with important character traits missing? Your life (and mine) may be the only Bible your neighbor ever reads. Nothing I do should shame the name "Christian." Could someone see that you are a Christian by your actions, or might someone think that you are obviously not a Christian?

2. To have a good name, we should always tell the whole truth. Psalm 15:1 and 2 says, *"LORD, who shall abide in thy tabernacle? who shall dwell in thy holy hill? He that walketh uprightly, and worketh righteousness, and speaketh the truth in his heart."* These verses teach to always be true to your word. God has a good name because He keeps His Word. If you promise that you will do something, then keep your commitment.

James 1:19 says, *"Wherefore, my beloved brethren, let every man be swift to hear, slow to speak, slow to wrath."* Do not carelessly make promises. Many times commitments are broken because we fail to check our schedules and think before we promise.

Ecclesiastes 5:2-5 admonishes, *"Be not rash with thy mouth, and let not thine heart be hasty to utter any thing before God: for God is in heaven, and thou upon earth: therefore let thy words be few. For a dream cometh through the multitude of business; and a fool's voice is known by multitude of words. When thou vowest a vow unto God, defer not to pay it; for he hath no pleasure in fools: pay that which thou hast vowed. Better is it that thou shouldest not vow, than that thou shouldest vow and not pay."* These verses also teach to keep your word to God and others. As I mentioned previously, God cannot lie; His reputation is intact. If someone placed a visible label on you that reflected your inside character, would you have a name of which you could be proud? Would your new name be "Miss Bitter" or "Miss Liar" or "Mr. Deceitful" or "Miss Gossip"? Be sure your label identifies you as a person of character — especially one who always tells the truth.

3. We are to bring honor to our parents' name. Ephesians 6:1-3 commands, *"Children, obey your parents in the Lord: for this is right. Honour thy father and mother; which is the first commandment with promise; That it may be well with thee, and thou mayest live long on the earth."* Honor your parents' name. Your last name should be a respected name.

Proverbs 28:7 teaches, *"Whoso keepeth the law is a wise son: but he that is a companion of riotous men shameth his father."* Parents work hard to build their name. Don't shame your father's reputation nor bring shame to your family name. Children have no right to mar their parents' name with wrong living. Live up to the honor of your name. If you happen to inherit a family name that lacks honor or does not seem to be a good one, then you should work to rebuild the reputation of that name during your generation.

4. To have a good name, don't hurt people to help yourself. Proverbs 1:18 and 19 says, *"And they lay wait for their own blood; they lurk privily for their own lives. So are the ways of every one that is greedy of gain; which taketh away the life of the owners thereof."* Today's frivolous lawsuits are part of the "get-rich-quick" philosophy of this generation. For instance, a nine-year-old broke into a home to steal, and, as a result, the homeowner's dog mauled the would-be thief. (Keep in mind that the homeowner was only trying to protect his property, which is his right according to the Constitution of the United States.) The boy's parents brought suit against the homeowner and were awarded $400,000.00 in court. In essence, the thief was rewarded, and the homeowner was penalized. I am sure that you would agree with me that this particular judgment was unethical. I believe that the family who brought suit will have a bad name. God teaches that a person hurts his name by taking advantage of others.

Playing the lottery and gambling, dispensing and drinking alcoholic beverages, selling and taking drugs, reading pornographic materials, and selling faulty products to elderly people are just a few ways to hurt your name. Counseling people for your own benefit is wrong also.

5. Your mate deserves to have a good name. Your spouse deserves to have a good name. Upon marriage, a wife takes her husband's name, and he must now live with her character helping or hurting his family name. A wife gives up her name to take the name of her husband. (At least, **submissive** wives do so!) Please make that name worthy. Sometimes I wonder if a couple would have been better off if he would have changed his last name to hers, based on the true character of his name. Your mate's reputation depends upon your character.

6. Be on time for everything, especially when making payments. Proverbs 3:27a says, *"Withhold not good from them to whom it is due."* Notice the words, *"it is due."* If a person contracted to be paid upon the completion of a project and payment is not made until the next day, that payment is **one day late**! Payments should be made when they are due. Don't take advantage of grace periods. I believe that grace period offenders are helping to destroy America. It is teaching a bad philosophy.

The size of the bill owed does not determine whether that amount needs to be paid on time or not. When you pay late, you hurt others. When you pay late, you can cause others to be late with their payments. Just because you are making a payment to a large corporation does not mean that company can carry your account. The company you owe must pay its debts on time also. Your late payment could give another company a bad name.

If your boss paid you late, you would probably quit. You would call him crooked — especially if your paycheck was several days late. That same statement is true of you if you do not pay your bills on time. Someone may not get to be paid because of you.

Always be on time for work and church. If you have an emergency, call ahead to tell them that you will be late. Always being late is a character flaw.

7. We should give our children an honored name. Proverbs 10:7 teaches, *"The memory of the just is blessed: but the name of the* *wicked shall rot."* Will your children rot because of the name you pass down to them? Your sinful lifestyle gives you a bad name about which you don't care. Think of your children. Your lifestyle may cause them to be labeled the same because of how you have lived.

Have you ever had to live down something that your older brother or sister did in school? This is another example of one hurting the name of another. What happens when your children seek a job where you work? Could they get hired because of their name, or would the story be the exact opposite?

8. To have a good name, return anything and everything which you borrow. Psalm 37:21 says, *"The wicked borroweth, and payeth not again: but the righteous sheweth mercy, and giveth."* To borrow and not return is unethical. Many times borrowing becomes stealing because the borrowed item is never returned. I can assure you that a lender never forgets the $5.00 he loaned, but the borrower often forgets easily. Some people honestly forget because they do not write down what they accept on loan, but forgetfulness does not forgive a debt. In essence, borrowing without returning is really stealing. "Borrow" is not a permanent term. The amount taken does not determine if stealing is a sin.

My dad always told me not to borrow anything that I could not afford to replace. When I wanted to borrow an item, he would ask, "Can you afford to replace it?" Often I would say, "Yes." He would then say, "Buy your own then and don't borrow." This philosophy may well be one of the surest ways to keep a good name.

9. To have a good name, keep your business dealings fair and above reproach. Proverbs 16:11 teaches, *"A just weight and balance are the LORD'S: all the weights of the bag are his work."* Some merchants of old would use three different sets of weights for buying and selling. They would unfairly substitute heavier weights when they were selling in order to make a profit; they would substitute lighter weights when purchasing to receive more also. If they were afraid to cheat a certain client or the scales and balances were checked, the merchants always had the proper set of weights to prove their "honesty."

Perhaps in your own way, you are like these dishonest merchants

CHARACTER

in your own personal dealings. Just be honest; do not try to hurt another. Are you dishonest when you have something to sell? When you sell a car, do you reset the odometer? Do you clean the engine so the oil leak won't be noticed? You wouldn't want a dealer to lie to you about the dependability of a car your wife will be driving. Your buyer has a wife about whom he cares also. Don't advertise dishonestly. Don't sell anything you know to be faulty. Honor all warranties that you give.

10. To have and keep a good name, spend time with others who have a good name. II Corinthians 6:17a commands the Christian, *"Wherefore come out from among them, and be ye separate, saith the Lord."* Proverbs 13:20 says, *"He that walketh with wise men shall be wise: but a companion of fools shall be destroyed."* Are your friends considered wise or foolish? It will always be true that if you play with pigs, you will smell like them. Fair or not, spending time with a person who has a bad name could give you a bad name.

11. Your name ought to be written in God's Book. If you are not saved, your name is **not** written in the Lamb's Book of Life. If you want to someday be called by the name "Christian," you must get saved. Once a person is saved, I might add that there are no erasure marks in this book. Please see Chapter 22 on "Character and Salvation" for help in knowing for sure that you are on your way to Heaven.

What Should Your Name Be?

My name is "Jeffery." The name "Jeffery" is merely a label my mother chose for the outside of me that should reflect my inward character. If your outside was renamed with your character description, what would your name be? The Bible gives some incidences of name changes. For instance, Naomi's name, meaning *pleasant*, was changed to Mara, meaning *bitter*. Jacob's name, meaning *trickster*, was changed to Israel, which means *power with God*.

Because of your character level, will your given name be changed by those who know you to a name meaning one of these attributes:

CHARACTER AND HAVING A GOOD NAME TO REFLECT IT

late, lazy, hasty, hateful, untrustworthy, liar; **or,** when people hear your name, will they think of a person whose name means one of the following: dependable, prompt, kind, considerate, faithful, or diligent? Labor to have a good name.

Chapter 9

Character and
Our God, a Perfect Example

OUR GOD IS A great God of character. Our God is the kind of God Who says what He means and means what He says. He is always on time. Our God never breaks His promises or His Word. *"For ever, O LORD, thy word is settled in heaven."* (Psalm 119:89) He has also promised that His Word will not return void. *"So shall my word be that goeth forth out of my mouth: it shall not return unto me void, but it shall accomplish that which I please, and it shall prosper in the thing whereto I sent it."* (Isaiah 55:11) God pledged to preserve His Word in Psalm 12:6 and 7 which says, *"The words of the LORD are pure words: as silver tried in a furnace of earth, purified seven times. Thou shalt keep them, O LORD, thou shalt preserve them from this generation for ever."* Everything God promised He would do, He did. *"I will worship toward thy holy temple, and praise thy name for thy lovingkindness and for thy truth."* (Psalm 138:2a) Everything God ever promised He would finish, He finished.

Let's look at some of the promises that God has made. Remember, He put His name on the line to make these promises. Each of these promises has been fulfilled, and that is why His name is above every name. *"Wherefore God also hath highly exalted him, and given him a name which is above every name."* (Philippians 2:9) Everything of which God speaks will come to pass. *"For I am the LORD: I will speak, and the word that I shall speak shall come to pass."* (Ezekiel 12:25a) **He is the perfect example of character and integrity.** Allow

CHARACTER

me to share some promises made by God in the Old Testament that were fulfilled in the New Testament.

THE PROMISE MADE BY GOD IN THE OLD TESTAMENT:
"Therefore the Lord himself shall give you a sign; Behold, a virgin shall conceive, and bear a son, and shall call his name Immanuel." (Isaiah 7:14)

NEW TESTAMENT FULFILLMENT OF THE PROMISE:
"Now the birth of Jesus Christ was on this wise: When as his mother Mary was espoused to Joseph, before they came together, she was found with child of the Holy Ghost. Then Joseph her husband, being a just man, and not willing to make her a publick example, was minded to put her away privily. But while he thought on these things, behold, the angel of the Lord appeared unto him in a dream, saying, Joseph, thou son of David, fear not to take unto thee Mary thy wife: for that which is conceived in her is of the Holy Ghost. And she shall bring forth a son, and thou shalt call his name JESUS: for he shall save his people from their sins. Now all this was done, that it might be fulfilled which was spoken of the Lord by the prophet, saying, Behold, a virgin shall be with child, and shall bring forth a son, and they shall call his name Emmanuel, which being interpreted is, God with us. Then Joseph being raised from sleep did as the angel of the Lord had bidden him, and took unto him his wife: And knew her not till she had brought forth her firstborn son: and he called his name JESUS."
(Matthew 1:18-25)

THE PROMISE MADE BY GOD IN THE OLD TESTAMENT:
"When Israel was a child, then I loved him, and called my son out of Egypt." (Hosea 11:1)

NEW TESTAMENT FULFILLMENT OF THE PROMISE:
"And when they were departed, behold, the angel of the Lord appeareth to Joseph in a dream, saying, Arise, and take the young child and his mother, and flee into Egypt, and be thou there until I bring thee word: for Herod will seek the young child to destroy him. When he arose, he took the young child and his mother by night, and departed into Egypt: And was there until the death of Herod: that it might be fulfilled which was spoken of

CHARACTER AND OUR GOD, A PERFECT EXAMPLE

the Lord by the prophet, saying, Out of Egypt have I called my son. Then Herod, when he saw that he was mocked of the wise men, was exceeding wroth, and sent forth, and slew all the children that were in Bethlehem, and in all the coasts thereof, from two years old and under, according to the time which he had diligently enquired of the wise men." (Matthew 2:13-16)

THE PROMISE MADE BY GOD IN THE OLD TESTAMENT:
"And I said unto them, If ye think good, give me my price; and if not, forbear. So they weighed for my price thirty pieces of silver. And the LORD said unto me, Cast it unto the potter: a goodly price that I was prised at of them. And I took the thirty pieces of silver, and cast them to the potter in the house of the LORD." (Zechariah 11:12, 13)

NEW TESTAMENT FULFILLMENT OF THE PROMISE:
"Then Judas, which had betrayed him, when he saw that he was condemned, repented himself, and brought again the thirty pieces of silver to the chief priests and elders, Saying, I have sinned in that I have betrayed the innocent blood. And they said, What is that to us? see thou to that. And he cast down the pieces of silver in the temple, and departed, and went and hanged himself. And the chief priests took the silver pieces, and said, It is not lawful for to put them into the treasury, because it is the price of blood. And they took counsel, and bought with them the potter's field, to bury strangers in. Wherefore that field was called, The field of blood, unto this day. Then was fulfilled that which was spoken by Jeremy the prophet, saying, And they took the thirty pieces of silver, the price of him that was valued, whom they of the children of Israel did value; And gave them for the potter's field, as the Lord appointed me." (Matthew 27:3-10)

THE PROMISE MADE BY GOD IN THE OLD TESTAMENT:
"For thou wilt not leave my soul in hell; neither wilt thou suffer thine Holy One to see corruption." (Psalm 16:10)

NEW TESTAMENT FULFILLMENT OF THE PROMISE:
"Whom God hath raised up, having loosed the pains of death: because it was not possible that he should be holden of it." (Acts 2:24)

CHARACTER

THE PROMISE MADE BY GOD IN THE OLD TESTAMENT:
"He keepeth all his bones: not one of them is broken." (Psalm 34:20)

NEW TESTAMENT FULFILLMENT OF THE PROMISE:
"When Jesus therefore had received the vinegar, he said, It is finished: and he bowed his head, and gave up the ghost. The Jews therefore, because it was the preparation, that the bodies should not remain upon the cross on the sabbath day, (for that sabbath day was an high day,) besought Pilate that their legs might be broken, and that they might be taken away. Then came the soldiers, and brake the legs of the first, and of the other which was crucified with him. But when they came to Jesus, and saw that he was dead already, they brake not his legs: But one of the soldiers with a spear pierced his side, and forthwith came there out blood and water. And he that saw it bare record, and his record is true: and he knoweth that he saith true, that ye might believe. For these things were done, that the scripture should be fulfilled, A bone of him shall not be broken." (John 19:30-36)

THE PROMISE MADE BY GOD IN THE OLD TESTAMENT:
"And he said, Go, and tell this people, Hear ye indeed, but understand not; and see ye indeed, but perceive not." (Isaiah 6:9)

NEW TESTAMENT FULFILLMENT OF THE PROMISE:
"Therefore speak I to them in parables: because they seeing see not; and hearing they hear not, neither do they understand. And in them is fulfilled the prophecy of Esaias, which saith, By hearing ye shall hear, and shall not understand; and seeing ye shall see, and shall not perceive."
(Matthew 13:13, 14)

THE PROMISE MADE BY GOD IN THE OLD TESTAMENT:
"Yea, mine own familiar friend, in whom I trusted, which did eat of my bread, hath lifted up his heel against me." (Psalm 41:9)

NEW TESTAMENT FULFILLMENT OF THE PROMISE:
"I speak not of you all: I know whom I have chosen: but that the scripture may be fulfilled, He that eateth bread with me hath lifted up his heel against me. Now I tell you before it come, that, when it is come to pass,

ye may believe that I am he ... When Jesus had thus said, he was troubled in spirit, and testified, and said, Verily, verily, I say unto you, that one of you shall betray me. Then the disciples looked one on another, doubting of whom he spake. Now there was leaning on Jesus' bosom one of his disciples, whom Jesus loved. Simon Peter therefore beckoned to him, that he should ask who it should be of whom he spake. He then lying on Jesus' breast saith unto him, Lord, who is it? Jesus answered, He it is, to whom I shall give a sop, when I have dipped it. And when he had dipped the sop, he gave it to Judas Iscariot, the son of Simon. And after the sop Satan entered into him. Then said Jesus unto him, That thou doest, do quickly. Now no man at the table knew for what intent he spake this unto him. For some of them thought, because Judas had the bag, that Jesus had said unto him, Buy those things that we have need of against the feast; or, that he should give something to the poor. He then having received the sop went immediately out: and it was night." (John 13:18-30)

THE PROMISE MADE BY GOD IN THE OLD TESTAMENT:
   "Therefore will I divide him a portion with the great, and he shall divide the spoil with the strong; because he hath poured out his soul unto death: and he was numbered with the transgressors; and he bare the sin of many, and made intercession for the transgressors." (Isaiah 53:12)

NEW TESTAMENT FULFILLMENT OF THE PROMISE:
   "And with him they crucify two thieves; the one on his right hand, and the other on his left. And the scripture was fulfilled, which saith, And he was numbered with the transgressors." (Mark 15:27, 28)

THE PROMISE MADE BY GOD IN THE OLD TESTAMENT:
   "But thou, Beth-lehem Ephratah, though thou be little among the thousands of Judah, yet out of thee shall he come forth unto me that is to be ruler in Israel; whose goings forth have been from of old, from everlasting." (Micah 5:2)

NEW TESTAMENT FULFILLMENT OF THE PROMISE:
   "Now when Jesus was born in Bethlehem of Judæa in the days of Herod

CHARACTER

the king, behold, there came wise men from the east to Jerusalem, Saying, Where is he that is born King of the Jews? for we have seen his star in the east, and are come to worship him. When Herod the king had heard these things, he was troubled, and all Jerusalem with him. And when he had gathered all the chief priests and scribes of the people together, he demanded of them where Christ should be born. And they said unto him, In Bethlehem of Judæa: for thus it is written by the prophet, And thou Bethlehem, in the land of Juda, art not the least among the princes of Juda: for out of thee shall come a Governor, that shall rule my people Israel." (Matthew 2:1-6)

THE PROMISE MADE BY GOD IN THE OLD TESTAMENT:
"And I will pour upon the house of David, and upon the inhabitants of Jerusalem, the spirit of grace and of supplications: and they shall look upon me whom they have pierced, and they shall mourn for him, as one mourneth for his only son, and shall be in bitterness for him, as one that is in bitterness for his firstborn." (Zechariah 12:10)

NEW TESTAMENT FULFILLMENT OF THE PROMISE:
"But one of the soldiers with a spear pierced his side, and forthwith came there out blood and water. And he that saw it bare record, and his record is true: and he knoweth that he saith true, that ye might believe. For these things were done, that the scripture should be fulfilled, A bone of him shall not be broken. And again another scripture saith, They shall look on him whom they pierced." (John 19:34-37)

THE PROMISE MADE BY GOD IN THE OLD TESTAMENT:
"They gave me also gall for my meat; and in my thirst they gave me vinegar to drink." (Psalm 69:21)

NEW TESTAMENT FULFILLMENT OF THE PROMISE:
"After this, Jesus knowing that all things were now accomplished, that the scripture might be fulfilled, saith, I thirst. Now there was set a vessel full of vinegar: and they filled a spunge with vinegar, and put it upon hyssop, and put it to his mouth." (John 19:28, 29)

CHARACTER AND OUR GOD, A PERFECT EXAMPLE

THE PROMISE MADE BY GOD IN THE OLD TESTAMENT:
"They part my garments among them, and cast lots upon my vesture." (Psalm 22:18)

NEW TESTAMENT FULFILLMENT OF THE PROMISE:
"And they crucified him, and parted his garments, casting lots: that it might be fulfilled which was spoken by the prophet, They parted my garments among them, and upon my vesture did they cast lots." (Matthew 27:35)

THE PROMISE MADE BY GOD IN THE OLD TESTAMENT:
"Rejoice greatly, O daughter of Zion; shout, O daughter of Jerusalem: behold, thy King cometh unto thee: he is just, and having salvation; lowly, and riding upon an ass, and upon a colt the foal of an ass." (Zechariah 9:9)

NEW TESTAMENT FULFILLMENT OF THE PROMISE:
"And when they drew nigh unto Jerusalem, and were come to Bethphage, unto the mount of Olives, then sent Jesus two disciples, Saying unto them, Go into the village over against you, and straightway ye shall find an ass tied, and a colt with her: loose them, and bring them unto me .... All this was done, that it might be fulfilled which was spoken by the prophet, saying, Tell ye the daughter of Sion, Behold, thy King cometh unto thee, meek, and sitting upon an ass, and a colt the foal of an ass. And the disciples went, and did as Jesus commanded them, And brought the ass, and the colt, and put on them their clothes, and they set him thereon. And a very great multitude spread their garments in the way; others cut down branches from the trees, and strawed them in the way. And the multitudes that went before, and that followed, cried, saying, Hosanna to the son of David: Blessed is he that cometh in the name of the Lord; Hosanna in the highest. And when he was come into Jerusalem, all the city was moved, saying, Who is this? And the multitude said, This is Jesus the prophet of Nazareth of Galilee." (Matthew 21:1-11)

THE PROMISE MADE BY GOD IN THE OLD TESTAMENT:
"The Spirit of the Lord GOD is upon me, because the LORD hath anointed me to preach good tidings unto the meek; he hath sent me to bind up the brokenhearted, to proclaim liberty to the captives, and the opening of

the prison to them that are bound; To proclaim the acceptable year of the LORD, and the day of vengeance of our God; to comfort all that mourn." (Isaiah 61:1, 2)

NEW TESTAMENT FULFILLMENT OF THE PROMISE:

"And he came to Nazareth, where he had been brought up: and, as his custom was, he went into the synagogue on the sabbath day, and stood up for to read. And there was delivered unto him the book of the prophet Esaias. And when he had opened the book, he found the place where it was written, The Spirit of the Lord is upon me, because he hath anointed me to preach the gospel to the poor; he hath sent me to heal the brokenhearted, to preach deliverance to the captives, and recovering of sight to the blind, to set at liberty them that are bruised, To preach the acceptable year of the Lord. And he closed the book, and he gave it again to the minister, and sat down. And the eyes of all them that were in the synagogue were fastened on him. And he began to say unto them, This day is this scripture fulfilled in your ears." (Luke 4:16-21)

THE PROMISE MADE BY GOD IN THE OLD TESTAMENT:

"I will open my mouth in a parable: I will utter dark sayings of old." (Psalm 78:2)

NEW TESTAMENT FULFILLMENT OF THE PROMISE:

"All these things spake Jesus unto the multitude in parables; and without a parable spake he not unto them: That it might be fulfilled which was spoken by the prophet, saying, I will open my mouth in parables; I will utter things which have been kept secret from the foundation of the world." (Matthew 13:34, 35)

It is evident that throughout eternity God has been unfailing at keeping His word. Therefore, the fulfillment of future events will prove Him to do the same. We can be sure that what He has promised for our future will be fulfilled because He is a God of great character. The character of God concerning the future will be proven in the following passages:

CHARACTER AND OUR GOD, A PERFECT EXAMPLE

"And this gospel of the kingdom shall be preached in all the world for a witness unto all nations; and then shall the end come." (Matthew 24:14)

"For our conversation is in heaven; from whence also we look for the Saviour, the Lord Jesus Christ: Who shall change our vile body, that it may be fashioned like unto his glorious body, according to the working whereby he is able even to subdue all things unto himself." (Philippians 3:20, 21)

"If ye then be risen with Christ, seek those things which are above, where Christ sitteth on the right hand of God. Set your affection on things above, not on things on the earth. For ye are dead, and your life is hid with Christ in God. When Christ, who is our life, shall appear, then shall ye also appear with him in glory." (Colossians 3:1-4)

"For if we believe that Jesus died and rose again, even so them also which sleep in Jesus will God bring with him. For this we say unto you by the word of the Lord, that we which are alive and remain unto the coming of the Lord shall not prevent them which are asleep. For the Lord himself shall descend from heaven with a shout, with the voice of the archangel, and with the trump of God: and the dead in Christ shall rise first: Then we which are alive and remain shall be caught up together with them in the clouds, to meet the Lord in the air: and so shall we ever be with the Lord." (I Thessalonians 4:14-17)

"And I saw thrones, and they sat upon them, and judgment was given unto them: and I saw the souls of them that were beheaded for the witness of Jesus, and for the word of God, and which had not worshipped the beast, neither his image, neither had received his mark upon their foreheads, or in their hands; and they lived and reigned with Christ a thousand years." (Revelation 20:4)

Chapter 10

Character
and
Seeking Counsel

THE BIBLE SAYS IN I Kings 3:16-28, *"Then came there two women, that were harlots, unto the king, and stood before him. And the one woman said, O my lord, I and this woman dwell in one house; and I was delivered of a child with her in the house. And it came to pass the third day after that I was delivered, that this woman was delivered also: and we were together; there was no stranger with us in the house, save we two in the house. And this woman's child died in the night; because she overlaid it. And she arose at midnight, and took my son from beside me, while thine handmaid slept, and laid it in her bosom, and laid her dead child in my bosom. And when I rose in the morning to give my child suck, behold, it was dead: but when I had considered it in the morning, behold, it was not my son, which I did bear. And the other woman said, Nay; but the living is my son, and the dead is thy son. And this said, No; but the dead is thy son, and the living is my son. Thus they spake before the king. Then said the king, The one saith, This is my son that liveth, and thy son is the dead: and the other saith, Nay; but thy son is the dead, and my son is the living. And the king said, Bring me a sword. And they brought a sword before the king. And the king said, Divide the living child in two, and give half to the one, and half to the other. Then spake the woman whose the living child was unto the king, for her bowels yearned upon her son, and she said, O my lord, give her the living child, and in no wise slay it. But the other said, Let it be*

CHARACTER

neither mine nor thine, but divide it. Then the king answered and said, Give her the living child, and in no wise slay it: she is the mother thereof. And all Israel heard of the judgment which the king had judged; and they feared the king: for they saw that the wisdom of God was in him, to do judgment."

I Kings 3:16-28 records a story in which two harlots came to King Solomon for his wisdom and discernment in settling a dispute. They had been living in the same house, and each had a young child. No other people were living in the house with them. During the night, one of the women accidentally smothered her child. She went to the mother of the living child who was sleeping and exchanged her dead baby for the living one. The next day both claimed the living baby.

They had to take this issue to Solomon. They stood before Solomon, and each gave her side of the story. In order to resolve the problem, Solomon called for a sword to divide the young child into two pieces — one for each mother. The actual mother pleaded for the baby's life and offered to give the child to the other woman, who said, *"Divide it."* No doubt Solomon had no question about who was the real mother. He saw the mother's love.

In this story, we find two harlots who were intelligent enough to seek counsel. Another point of significance in the story of these immoral women was the fact that they had the character to seek counsel from a wise man of God. I find that people who seek counsel are usually people of character and wisdom. By seeking counsel, a person will benefit in two ways: (1) he will receive direction for developing more character; (2) he will learn with the help of a counselor how **not** to destroy the character he has already gained.

Because the Bible gives many instances of people needing and seeking counsel, let me share some principles I have learned which have helped me to be open to counsel.

1. **Do not be guilty of never seeking counsel.** Proverbs 11:14 says, *"Where no counsel is, the people fall: but in the multitude of counsellors there is safety."* Deuteronomy 32:28 says, *"For they are a nation void of counsel, neither is there any understanding in them."* These two verses teach the importance of seeking counsel. Remember, even the two harlots showed enough wisdom to seek counsel in order

CHARACTER AND SEEKING COUNSEL

to settle their dispute. If two women, obviously living in sin, went to a man of God for counsel, should not Christians receive counsel too?

However, some Christians never seek counsel. Never seeking counsel means trouble. At one time or another every person needs to seek counsel. I have found that most, if not every person who leaves God's will, left it because they never sought or received counsel. People with character seek counsel.

So why do some Christians never seek counsel? I believe there are two main reasons for never seeking or receiving counsel.

    a. **Because you plan to counsel yourself.** This is certainly not best, nor is it enough. The following three verses adequately explain why. Job 18:7b tells me, *"His own counsel shall cast him down."* Jeremiah 7:24a says, *"But they hearkened not,...but walked in the counsels and in the imagination of their evil heart, and went backward, and not forward."* Seeking and trusting your own counsel will take you backward. Psalm 5:10b says, *"Let them fall by their own counsels."* You may choose to counsel yourself, but the result is usually self-destruction.

    b. **Because you feel that if you ask for help with a problem, your weakness will be revealed.** Perhaps you think that after you reveal your weakness to a leader, you will lose future opportunities. Perhaps you believe the counselor will hold your weakness against you. After seeking counsel, you often leave with answers to your problems. The truth is that you are actually more qualified to lead after receiving and following counsel than before you sought advice.

When a person seeks counsel, he is better qualified for leadership, not less qualified. People who seek counsel usually become excellent leaders. The Bible gives a record of only one Person Who needed no counsel and was a success. Isaiah 40:13 and 14 says, *"Who hath directed the Spirit of the LORD, or being his counsellor hath taught him? With whom took he counsel, and who instructed him, and taught him in the path of judgment, and taught him knowledge, and shewed to him the way of understanding?"* If you don't think you need any

CHARACTER

counsel, you must presume you are God because He is the only One Who has never needed counsel from anybody. You are your own god. Never seeking or accepting counsel can be equated with having no character.

2. Do not be guilty of seeking unwise counsel. Psalm 1:1a teaches, *"Blessed is the man that walketh not in the counsel of the ungodly."* Job 22:18b says, *"The counsel of the wicked is far from me."* Proverbs 12:5b informs us that, *"The counsels of the wicked are deceit."* Christians should seek counsel from seasoned, older, and wiser people.

In I Kings 12:8-13, the account of Rehoboam seeking counsel from the young men instead of the old men is given; and, as a result of his lack of discernment, he split the kingdom. I'm sure Rehoboam didn't think the counsel he received would be so detrimental to his people. The same is true of Christians today. Receiving and accepting unwise counsel could cause a church split or a divided family or even division in one's own home. Why? Bad counsel was sought, accepted, and followed! The reason some Christians seek counsel from people their own age is because they don't want truthful and right counsel. They want someone who will agree with them so that they may do whatever they please.

Accepting and following unwise counsel brings tragedy. *"Behold, these caused the children of Israel, through the counsel of Balaam, to commit trespass against the LORD in the matter of Peor, and there was a plague among the congregation of the LORD."* (Numbers 31:16) According to I Chronicles 10:13, accepting bad counsel caused Saul's death. Accepting and following unwise counsel usually ends in devastation. Another result of listening to unwise counsel is a low character level.

3. Seek counsel from the wise person as often as necessary. Proverbs 13:20a teaches, *"He that walketh with wise men shall be wise."* The Bible says in Proverbs 4:7a that *"Wisdom is the principal thing."* This verse means that the obtaining of wisdom is urgent. One way to obtain wisdom is by seeking counsel from wise people as often as necessary. Wisdom for man is being able to see life the way in which God sees it. The two harlots of I Kings 3 sought counsel in

CHARACTER AND SEEKING COUNSEL

order to settle a conflict. Surely you would want to have as much wisdom as these harlots displayed in seeking counsel. One person from whom counsel should be sought is a soul winner. In Proverbs 11:30 the Bible says, *"The fruit of the righteous is a tree of life; and he that winneth souls is wise."*

A person I deem wise once said to me, "Before I preach, I run. My whole goal is to get my heart pumping to get my blood circulating to help get the fresh oxygen from my lungs to my brain. When I step into the pulpit, I'm fresh! My mind is keener and sharper."

After considering this man's practice of running before preaching, I decided that I would do the same thing. Before I go to the pulpit and preach, every time I have the opportunity I go soul winning and try to get somebody saved. Why? I want to get **the** blood flowing! I am speaking of the blood of Christ. There is nothing that will give a preacher more confidence when walking into a pulpit than having won someone to Christ — having caused the blood to flow! Get your counsel from soul winners and people who believe in the death, burial, and resurrection of Christ and from those who share that good news with others.

I believe the only stupid question is the unasked question. I have four children. Since they were little they have asked me, "Why, Daddy?" I hope that my oldest boy Jeff, who is now 11 years old, will still ask at 14, "Why, Daddy?" I hope that when he is 18 he still says, "Why, Daddy?" When he is 21, I hope he will say, "Teach me, Dad. Help me to develop my character."

4. Characterless people have no counsel to offer and will find few people who will trust them.

5. A counselor with no character may have good sense and he may talk a good talk, but he cannot walk a good walk.

"Where no counsel is, the people fall."
(Proverbs 11:14a)

Chapter 11

Character and Reading the Bible

FIRST, WE NEED TO stop and realize that the Bible is the **Word of God**. On the surface you say and believe that the Bible is God's Word, but I wonder if that conviction goes any deeper than just the surface? God has something for you in the Bible; therefore, He wants you to study the Bible daily. However, do you know how most of us are? We get excited about somebody who is excited about the Bible. We get excited when we hear a new truth delivered from the pulpit. In other words, we get excited about the excitement.

I would like for you to be able to get excited about the One Who excites. Have you ever wished that you could truly get excited about your Bible reading? If you are even a halfway decent Christian and you'll be honest, you are saying, "Yes, I would *love* to get excited about the Bible, but that doesn't seem to happen to me."

A long time ago I decided that if having personal devotions was worth doing, it was worth doing right. *I believe you can get excited about God, and you can have a devotional time with God that is exciting and productive and real. You can go away from your personal devotions saying, "WOW! That was good. I needed that. That will help me."*

Just like everything else of value in life, this success will be achieved by having personal character. If you will by character do the following, your Bible reading will be transformed. The following six steps are those I take every time I open my Bible to have my personal

CHARACTER

Bible devotions.

1. By character, come to the Word of God expecting to get something from the time you spend with Him. When it is time for me to have my personal devotions, I begin to think about what the Book is. I approach my devotions by faith because the Bible very clearly teaches that faith comes by hearing and hearing by the Word of God. (You thought the only purpose for faith in this life was to get money!) Therefore, what would be wrong with practicing faith when it comes to reading the Word of God? I read my Bible in faith, believing that I will receive something from it; I believe that *something* is going to happen as a result of my reading.

Many of you walk away from reading your Bible and feel the following, "I didn't get anything out of that." Probably you didn't believe that anything was going to happen in the first place! You will practice having faith in everything except for the Word of God, yet the Word of God is that in which you ought to practice the most faith!

I look at my Bible and say, "I'm going to get something out of that when I read it." Think about it: Does *God* want you to get something from your devotions? Does *God* have a truth for you? Does *God* want to bless you? Does *God* want the Holy Spirit to speak to your heart in your devotions? Yes, of course He does! You, by faith, must believe that the Almighty God of the universe wants to show you a truth!

That which is not done by faith is sin. Can you read your Bible and be sinning? Start believing that you are going to get something from your Bible-reading time, and be open to the truth He has especially for you.

2. By character, come surrendering to the truths that God reveals to you. *I plan to change before the command to change.* I go to God and say, "God, I know I'm about to learn something You have for me. I just want You to know right now that whatever You want me to do — I will do it! I don't even have to know what it is, God. You don't even have to tell me in advance what You are going to teach me and tell me to do."

How much sense does it make for someone to say that they want something, yet once they receive it not use it? That is poor character.

CHARACTER AND READING THE BIBLE

What did you do with the last truth that you were given? God is not in a hurry to give more truth to somebody who abused the last one they were given.

3. By character, I come expecting to use the truth that God has given me. At this point in my devotion time, I have still not opened my Bible yet to begin reading. Promise God you will take what He is about to give you and share it. I share what God gives me with my wife and my children. "Whatever You give me, I'm going to give it away. I'll not hoard your truths to myself. I will not read it and reject it; I'm going to do something with it." Do you know the greatest gift you could give is the truth of God?

Some of you need to approach your Bible reading with the realization that when you read and reject a truth, you could be hurting many. You are rejecting the benefit that anyone would have received who would have come under the sound of that truth if you had accepted and given away the truth. *Most of us are spiritually educated beyond our character to perform.* I promise God that I will be a conduit of the truth. I promise God that if He will show me His truths, I will rush it to others. You won't find me keeping a stockpile of truth.

Let me ask you a question: To whom are you giving the truth? The most important gift you can give anybody is the truth. Because you are not a conduit, you have been wasting your devotional time.

4. By character, do not be in a hurry. I often think the way most Christians treat our God is amazing. We are always in a hurry. Let me show you how many approach their devotion time.

> *"Okay, God. You've got two minutes to bless me. Let's get this over with; come on, hurry up, God."*

I believe if you will be reasonable in scheduling your time with God, He will give you some truths within that frame of time. You may say, "God, I'll meet You at 7:00 a.m., and God, I **am** going to meet You."

Let me ask you a question: If you had an appointment with your pastor that began at 7:00 a.m., would you want to be late? Would you

CHARACTER

be late to an appointment with a heart specialist if you were experiencing shortness of breath? Of course not. Do you go to your appointments with God with the same kind of respect? I wonder how many times God showed up for the appointment, but you didn't?

Some Christians take more time to eat a sandwich than they do with the Bread they were given from God. They wonder why they are miserable. I believe God would meet your timetable if you would just show up.

I recommend that you set up a schedule and have your devotions at the same time every day. If you do so, you are more apt to follow your schedule. I believe some of you will have a very difficult time being around God in Heaven because you only have a couple of minutes every now and then for Him on earth. When you get to Heaven and everybody is spending the first 100 million years around the throne, you will be looking at your watch thinking, "Ah, great. I've far exceeded my two-minute time limit. Is there anything else to do up here?"

5. By character, come for the right reason. Come to your time with God with the proper emphasis; come to glorify Him. I am to magnify God. You ought to realize that in **not** obeying and **not** having your devotions and in **not** reading in your Bible and in **not** approaching it God's way, He is not being glorified. Your life should be becoming holy and clean so He will receive the glory. Read God's Word for God's sake, not just your own.

6. By character, come to it, even if nothing *apparently* comes from your coming. The word "apparently" is the key word in this step. You say, "Brother Owens, I read my Bible, and I don't get anything out of it." You are wrong! You cannot tell me that your inability to comprehend what you received means that you received nothing. The Word of God is more powerful than that. *"For the word of God is quick, and powerful, and sharper than any twoedged sword, piercing even to the dividing asunder of soul and spirit, and of the joints and marrow, and is a discerner of the thoughts and intents of the heart."* (Hebrews 4:12) Never underestimate the power of the Word of God.

After my first son Jeffery was born, he was placed in the nursery

CHARACTER AND READING THE BIBLE

at the hospital. The very first day he was born, I took my New Testament and placed it against the nursery window and said to him through the glass, "Jeffery, this is the Word of God. This is the Word of God." From the first day my children were born, we have had devotions with them every day of their lives. From the time our children were small, I would play the Bible on cassette tapes to them in their bassinets for hours. You say, "Brother Owens, do you really think that helped?" Do you mean to tell me that you really think it didn't help?

My kids have devotions every day. Many people no longer believe in family devotions, but I still do. The reason many people do not believe in them is because they do not have the character to stay home long enough to have devotions with their families. I believe we always get something from the Word of God, whether or not we think we do. Let me illustrate it with this story.

A young man from the city was visiting a farm. The old farmer said to him, "I want you to take this wicker basket to the creek at the bottom of the hill and fill the basket with water. Then, bring it back to me." Wanting to please the farmer, the young man grabbed the basket, ran with all his might to the creek where he dipped the basket into the creek, filled it, and carried it back to the top of the hill. However, by the time the young man reached the old man, his basket was empty. The old man calmly said, "Do it again." So the young man ran to the bottom of the hill, dipped the basket deep into the water, pulled it out, and ran quickly to the top of the hill, but the basket was empty. Once more the old man said, "Fill it again."

With all the determination he could muster, the boy said, "I'll dip the basket as deep as it can be dipped. I'll bring the basket back filled with water, or I'll die trying." The young man ran to the bottom of the hill. He dipped the basket deep. He ran with all of his might; but when he reached the top of the hill, the basket was empty. He disgustedly threw the basket down and said, "Old man, you're humiliating me. I've tried three times, and I can't keep water in the basket. You're wasting my time. I'm not getting anything out of this!"

The old man looked at the young man and softly said, "Young man, you have a clean basket."

You may say, "Brother Owens, I've been reading my Bible, and I'm not getting anything out of it." I contend that you are wrong in your assessment. Read it! It's cleansing you! It's doing something that you cannot imagine! All those times you read out of character and obedience, God was "dipping you deep into the Word, and you were coming up cleaner." Perhaps you felt like you were not "holding any water." You had better thank God that the Word of God is more powerful than your ability to comprehend what it is doing. *The Bible is the Word of God.* Come to the Bible and read it, even when nothing **apparently** comes from your coming. You cannot afford not to come to the Word of God on a daily basis.

Chapter 12

Character and Our Burdens

IN EXODUS 5:1-4 THE BIBLE says, *"And afterward Moses and Aaron went in, and told Pharaoh, Thus saith the LORD God of Israel, Let my people go, that they may hold a feast unto me in the wilderness. And Pharaoh said, Who is the LORD, that I should obey his voice to let Israel go? I know not the LORD, neither will I let Israel go. And they said, The God of the Hebrews hath met with us: let us go, we pray thee, three days' journey into the desert, and sacrifice unto the LORD our God; lest he fall upon us with pestilence, or with the sword. And the king of Egypt said unto them, Wherefore do ye, Moses and Aaron, let the people from their works? get you unto your burdens."*

In this chapter, let's consider the words of the last phrase, *"get you unto your burdens."* In this passage, the children of Israel were in captivity in Egypt. God knew His children were being abused; He knew they were not being fed enough; He knew they were not being clothed properly. He was well aware of their heavy burden. Pharaoh, their captor, knew they were hurting and inflicted greater injustices. When Moses and Aaron came to Pharaoh and said, "Let the people go," I believe, by the leadership of the Holy Spirit, Pharaoh answered, *"Get back to your burden."*

I'm sure some of the Israelites said, "But God, don't You understand what we are going through? Don't You understand how hard it is?" I'm sure someone declared, "God, this isn't fair," to which

CHARACTER

God responded, "I am always fair." Someone might have said, "God, You're not just!" God replied, "I am always just. Get back to your burden."

Let me illustrate by means of a story I once heard. An ant left his anthill in order to build a structure of wood. The ant thought, "To build this structure, I will need a stick of certain length and weight." So the ant began to search for that particular stick. He traveled through grass for hours. Remember, grass to an ant is like a tropical rain forest or a jungle. However, the ant could not find that specific stick that he needed. Soon the ant finished the trek through the "jungle" and came to a sidewalk. Remember, to humans, a sidewalk is simply a concrete path; to an ant, the sidewalk was like a freeway. Soon the ant left the "freeway" and went off into a sandy lot. To humans, it was just a vacant lot full of sand; to an ant, it was the hot, dry, and vast Sahara Desert. It was difficult to walk in the sand. Still, the ant searched and searched.

The ant did not think he would ever find exactly what he needed. The ant happened to look to his right, and he spotted a stick — the perfect stick! It was an old, used matchstick which someone had thrown on the ground. The ant thought, "This is exactly what I need!"

Then the ant looked at the sky and noticed the sun was going down. He thought to himself, "Oh, no, I've got to get back to the anthill. I cannot stay out here during the night. I must journey back across the desert and back across the freeway and into that jungle. I cannot possibly make it before dark. What am I going to do?"

The ant picked up that big matchstick and put it on his back. Of course, you know an ant can carry burdens that are many times its weight. How that match burdened him down! "It took me all day to get this far without a load. How long will it take me to get back home with this heavy weight on my back? What am I going to do?" the ant contemplated.

The ant began to search the horizon, and he saw something very familiar — a red brick fence. "I've seen that fence somewhere before. I believe that fence ends right by my anthill." This fence was eight feet high. Eight feet to humans was thousands of feet to the ant. But the fence was uniquely made; it began with an incline. The ant

CHARACTER AND OUR BURDENS

thought, "I can climb up that slant, and I will get on top of that fence. Then I can bypass that desert, that freeway, and the jungle. I can get my stick back to my anthill, and I can build what God wants me to build."

So the ant began to journey up that slope. He walked, and, oh, was that stick heavy! He had traveled across the top of that fence about two-thirds of the way when he came to where the mortar was missing between two bricks. To humans, it was a one-half inch gap that needed repair; to the ant, it was the Grand Canyon of Arizona. "Oh, now all the work that I have done is in vain. I am not going to make it back after all! I have carried this heavy burden for nothing."

The ant sat in contemplation. "I know exactly what to do." The ant removed the matchstick from his back and laid it across the gap between the two bricks. The ant cautiously walked across his stick to the other side. Then the ant picked up his burden and went on his way. Do you realize what this fable teaches? *The ant allowed his burden to become a bridge, and that is exactly what God wants His people to do with every burden they ever carry.*

Obviously, we do not all live in the same kind of a house. We do not all come from the same state, nor do we all look alike. However, there is one way that every person has something in common — every person has a burden. God looks down from Heaven today, and He says, "Take your burden. Accept your burden. Make it into a bridge."

1. The heavier your burden is, the stronger your bridge needs to be. Had the ant in this fable been carrying a blade of grass, it surely would have been a lighter load. But what if he had laid that piece of grass over his "Grand Canyon"? When he walked out onto that grass, he would have fallen because that blade of grass would not have supported him.

God will never allow a burden to come into your life that will destroy you. God permits burdens to come because He knows they will help shape you into a greater vessel for His service. You say, "I cannot take what I'm going through." God knows you can carry the burden He gave you. *"There hath no temptation taken you but such as is common to man: but God is faithful, who will not suffer you to be tempted above that ye are able; but will with the temptation also*

CHARACTER

make a way to escape, that ye may be able to bear it." (I Corinthians 10:13) If you are carrying a heavy burden, that means God trusts you, and He has a big bridge for you to build. Consider your burdens as building supplies.

One Sunday morning a lady in a wheelchair attended my Sunday school class of young married couples. I began to talk with her and found that she was in a wheelchair because of multiple sclerosis. She said, "Brother Owens, I have lost the use of my legs. Now I am losing the use of my arms. I have a little boy at home. My husband drinks, and he has left me because he can't take having an invalid wife. Why are these things happening to me? I am so very, very weak."

I answered, "No, you have it all wrong. You are so very, very strong. God knows you can take these burdens and heartaches. God knows you have something great to do, and you have to carry a heavy burden if you are going to build a strong bridge."

One of the verses in the song "Do, Lord" uses these words: "The heavier the cross, the brighter the crown." God would not ask someone to carry heavy burdens or heavy building supplies unless He had designed a blueprint for a beautiful bridge. He's the Architect, and you are His contractor. Your bridge will be magnificent. God knows exactly what He is doing. The heavier your burden, the greater your potential for building more character.

2. Let your burden be a bridge to your success. Mr. Dan Wolfe, a dear friend of mine, has a hook in the place of an arm. When Brother Wolfe was a young boy, his father owned a pizza parlor. Their pizzas were homemade; they ground their own meat and cheese. When Dan was six years old, he was in the basement with one of the employees, who was shredding the cheese for the pizza. Dan was sitting on the counter next to the grinder, and he had his hand over the mouth of the grinder. The employee flipped on the grinder switch without looking. Dan's hand was sucked into the grinder. Dan's father ripped the grinder off the counter and rushed him to the hospital. The doctors had to surgically remove that grinder from Dan's hand. Dan ended up being in the hospital for five months, and he had his hand and forearm cut off five more times to stop the spread of infection. When right-handed Dan regained his strength, his dad helped him

CHARACTER AND OUR BURDENS

learn to do everything left-handed. He could have sat back and whined and complained. Not Dan Wolfe! By the time he was in high school, he was on the high school basketball team scoring 20-30 points a game. He was high-point man on the team, even though he had only one hand. Last year I watched him coach junior varsity basketball. Dan didn't let his burden stop him; he built a bridge.

I attended public school. The hardest years of my life were my last three years in high school. Sometimes I practically had to fight to carry my Bible. One day when going to my geography class, five thugs met me at the door. "Hey, Preacher boy, are you taking your Bible to class?"

"Yes, I'm taking my Bible."

"You may be going to class, but your Bible is not going with you," they sneered.

"My Bible's going, and so am I."

They taunted, "You're going to have to go in through us."

"I don't care how I go in; I'm going in." About that time, one of them shoved me. Then another shoved me, and they tried to knock my Bible out of my hand. The pushing and shoving continued. That was quite a confrontation — five against one.

I played basketball for my high school team, and my coach basically despised me. When he used my name, it was almost like he was using profanity. He treated me so because I would not practice on Wednesday nights or Saturdays. I was a Christian, and on Wednesday night I belonged in church; on Saturdays I visited on my church bus route.

One night during a game I was sitting on the bench, and the coach was so used to yelling at me that as I sat on the bench beside him he began to yell, "Hey! Get on the ball out there, Owens. Let's go, let's go, let's go." I said, "Coach, I'm right here beside you. I'm not even on the court."

While I was in the public school, I started a Teenage Bible Club. The teenagers who wanted to could meet weekly just like a Spanish Club or a Chess Club. The name of my Bible Club was the Proverbs Club. We used the acrostic "T.R.O.T.," which meant **T**eens **R**eaching **O**ther **T**eens. Some of the students even used that name as a source

CHARACTER

of contention. Every day when I would go to the lunchroom, I had to walk down a long corridor. On both sides of the hallway were benches where all my so-called "friends" sat. When I walked through the hallway, they would begin chanting, "Trot, Billy Bible, trot." I had to walk through there every day as it seemed like my whole school tried to humiliate me.

I went to my preacher and said, "That's it! I've had it! I don't have to put up with this!"

"Jeff, you will graduate in four months."

I couldn't even think of graduating. All I could think of was the daily indignities. I said, "I should not have to go through that every day."

My preacher said, "Well, if you can't take it, I understand. What you're saying, Jeff, is that they're tougher than you."

"That's not what I'm saying, Preacher."

"In other words, they win, you lose?"

I said, "No, Preacher, that's not what I said."

Then my preacher said, "In other words, you're washing out? Jeff, I think you ought to quit."

"I'm not quitting, and you can't make me!" I retorted.

I went back to school and finished the hardest years of my life! There were 800 people in my school, and they laughed, mocked, scorned, and teased. At 17 years of age, I couldn't understand. I now can grasp why I had to face that hurt and humiliation. Five years ago, I figured out why. Five years ago, Brother Hyles called me into his office and said, "Jeff, I want you to become an assistant pastor here at First Baptist Church. I want you to direct a ministry called the Bible Club Ministry for public school teens."

From that time until this, I have had the privilege of seeing thousands upon thousands upon thousands of teenagers saved. We now have 18 Bible Clubs started all over the Hammond area. Bible Clubs are being started all across America. There are Bible Clubs in Canada and in Puerto Rico and in Mexico and in Australia. I receive letters from around the world about Bible Clubs.

I can tell you where the Bible Club Ministry started. It started when I was 16 years old and I carried a Bible to school with me and

CHARACTER AND OUR BURDENS

I remember saying, "God, it doesn't seem fair. I try to serve You. I don't understand, but I will keep on going. I don't know if I can bear that burden." Today I receive invitations to speak all over America and in foreign countries. God knew what my future would hold. God had not forgotten about me when I was struggling in high school; God had not betrayed me. Carrying your burden will develop your character, which will lead to success.

3. If you build a bridge with your burden, it will be a bridge for others. Galatians 6:2 says, *"Bear ye one another's burdens, and so fulfil the law of Christ."* The father of a young lady in Bible college came to pick her up for a holiday. On the way home, he attempted to rape her. Thank God, his evil intentions were halted. Upon her return, she came to me for counsel. She wept and said, "It's not fair!"

I said to her, "Look, God knows where you are. Do something with what you have learned from this experience." I saw her recently working with a Bible Club teenage girl whose father had tried to rape her. That heartbroken young lady made her burden a bridge. Always remember that somebody — a little brother, a little sister, a friend, a teen — will need to cross your bridge.

When I was a boy, I remember suffering and hurting though the divorces of many immediate family members. I can remember time and time again going to my room and crying and saying, "Lord, it's not right." Now I know why I had to watch this pain and suffering with a feeling of helplessness. When Dr. Jack Hyles hired me as an assistant pastor, he said, "I want you to work with young married couples." God knew that he needed someone who hated divorce and the problems caused by divorce. Believe me, I hate divorce with a passion. My greatest desire is to see people get married and stay married. Let me assure you, if you have been unfortunate enough to experience a divorce, I care about you and I hurt for you, but I hate what has happened to you.

4. Jesus was a bridge builder. God looked down from Heaven and said, "There are some people who are going to go to Hell down there. We must do something. I need a special bridge builder." So Jesus Christ came from a perfect Heaven to a sin-cursed world and

CHARACTER

lived 33 perfect, sinless, holy years. He was handed a piece of wood. He put it upon His back, and He began to carry it up Golgotha's hill. At the top of the hill, He was nailed to that piece of wood. He hung there, and He died. Three days later He took hold of that "matchstick" and said, "Here is the bridge. Everybody who wants to can go to Heaven. This is the bridge back to God — the bridge for all mankind to be saved."

Build your character by using your burden as a tool. Make your burden a bridge. Who's going to come across your bridge?

"Building the Bridge for Him"
by W. A. Dromgoole

An old man, travelling a lone highway
Came at the evening cold and gray
To a chasm deep and wide.

The old man crossed in the twilight dim,
For the sullen stream held no fears for him;
But he turned when he reached the other side,
And builded a bridge to span the tide.

"Old man," cried a fellow pilgrim near,
"You are wasting your strength with building here;
Your journey will end with the ending of day,
And you never again will pass this way.

"You have crossed the chasm deep and wide.
Why build you a bridge at eventide?"
And the builder raised his old gray head:
"There followed after me today
A youth whose feet will pass this way.

This stream, which has been as naught to me,
To that fair-haired boy may a pitfall be;
He, too, must cross in the twilight dim —
Good friend, I am building this bridge for him!"

Chapter 13

Character and Diligence

COLOSSIANS 3:23 SAYS, *"And whatsoever ye do, do it heartily, as to the Lord, and not unto men."* Diligence is performing every task as though done directly for the Lord. We must realize that our increase comes from Him and that we do all that we do for Him. Therefore, every task is worthy of our diligence.

In Colossians 3:23 consider the words, *"do it heartily."* These three words mean *put your heart into it.* Work your heart in two ways — as a physical organ in the body pumping blood, as well as having a heart's desire emotionally to work hard.

Also consider the phrase, *"as to the Lord, and not unto men."* This wording means to do your work, knowing that even if man can't always see you, God can. To please a finite, limited human being is usually easy, but to please an unlimited God is a constant challenge.

Examples of Diligent People

Jesse Owens was the son of a sharecropper in Alabama. Jesse was known as the "runt of the town," and was often teased about his physical size. In high school, he won an AAU long jump championship and won a scholarship to Ohio State University. At the 1936 Olympic games held in Berlin, Germany, Jesse Owens won four gold medals. He was just a little guy with a big character trait called diligence.

CHARACTER

Florence Nightingale was born on May 12, 1820, to wealthy parents who were vacationing in Florence, Italy. Her family divided their time between two estates in England. The Nightingales' fondest dream for their daughter was to marry into wealth. Florence wrote on February 7, 1837, that "God spoke to me and called me to His service." She felt God's purpose for her was caring for the sick. In the 1800's, public nurses were women of such low character that they were not discussed in front of proper young ladies. The hospitals were filthy houses to which the poor were taken to die.

Though her social position was a hindrance to her call to nursing, she overcame the obstacles. Florence Nightingale made of nursing a noble profession. She said, "Nursing is an art, and if it is to be made an art, it requires as exclusive a devotion, as hard preparation, as any painter's or sculptor's work; for what is having to do with dead canvas or cold marble compared with having to do with the living body — the temple of God's spirit." It has been said that the three people who did the most to alleviate human suffering in the 19th century were the inventor of antiseptic, the inventor of chloroform, and the nurse of nurses, Florence Nightingale, a woman of diligence.

Abraham Lincoln was the son of a drifter. Abraham worked as a store clerk for a while, but the store failed. He bought a partnership in another store, but it failed also. He ran for the legislature and lost. He ran for senator twice and lost both times. He ran for Vice-President and lost. He became the 16th President of the United States of America. In spite of failure, he was a man who was diligent.

Dr. Albert Einstein was termed a "slow learner." A teacher even recommended that he be withdrawn from school because of this deficiency. He tried to go to school in Switzerland but failed the entrance exam. He was fired from three teaching jobs. At the age of 26, he won the Nobel prize and spent the rest of his life setting a new standard for the world's scientific knowledge. Though he did poorly in school, Einstein is remembered as a genius today because of his diligence.

Dr. George Washington Carver was born a slave and had to educate himself. Because of the color of his skin, he was not allowed to attend school. His skin color would have been a hindrance to

CHARACTER AND DILIGENCE

others, but not to him. He amazed a skeptical group of congressmen by showing them, as a result of his studies, 145 useful products made from the peanut. In spite of the color of his skin, he rescued the economically impoverished South from destitution. Diligence is not based on skin color.

Marshall Field was the son of a Massachusetts farmer. At the age of 15, he went to work in a store as a clerk. The store owner soon told Marshall's father, "That boy of yours will never learn to keep store in a thousand years." Marshall Field proved the statement wrong. The young man, via his diligence, worked long hours and founded a world-famous retail store and publishing empire.

Of course, by now you can ascertain that all of these people had at least one trait in common. Jesse Owens was an athlete. Florence Nightingale was a nurse. Abraham Lincoln was a politician. Albert Einstein was a scientist. Dr. George Washington Carver was a teacher. Marshall Field was a businessman. Their one trait in common — diligence.

Jesse Owens was just a little guy who was often teased because of his size, but he was diligent in his desire to excel! Florence Nightingale's parents would have kept their daughter from her life's calling, but she was diligent in seeking God's will! Abraham Lincoln failed at nearly everything he attempted, but he was diligent to keep on trying. Dr. Albert Einstein did poorly in school, but he was diligent in his scientific research. George Washington Carver was black, but he was diligent in educating himself. Marshall Field was assessed a failure, but his diligence proved the prediction wrong.

Rewards of Diligence

The following six statements are some of the many benefits of being diligent.

1. Diligence brings you to the attention of the right people. Proverbs 22:29 says, *"Seest thou a man diligent in his business? he shall stand before kings; he shall not stand before mean men."* It is not your talent that is significant; it is your diligence that is most important. An employer will notice your hard work, and this will result in increased opportunity. Politicking and struggling for power is not necessary when a person is diligent.

2. Diligence may bring a better financial situation. Proverbs 10:4 says, *"He becometh poor that dealeth with a slack hand: but the hand of the diligent maketh rich."* You may think, "I will never have money for a secure future." This verse teaches that money is not the key, diligence is. Be sure that you work as unto Him. The Bible says in Psalm 50:10, *"For every beast of the forest is mine, and the cattle upon a thousand hills."*

3. Diligence increases your ability to think well. Proverbs 21:5 says, *"The thoughts of the diligent tend only to plenteousness; but of every one that is hasty only to want."* You may think, "I just don't think clearly." Be diligent! God has several rewards for being diligent, one of which is clear thinking. When you are diligent, God will give you a mind that is creative and full of ideas. Lazy people don't think well. Have you noticed that the person who is most diligent on a project is the one who has many ideas? I believe this is no accident or coincidence.

4. Diligent people often get to lead. Proverbs 12:24 teaches, *"The hand of the diligent shall bear rule: but the slothful shall be under tribute."* If you are diligent, and even if you do not receive a position of authority, you have definitely achieved the character of authority. This is to be commended.

5. Diligence will help you to reach your goals. Proverbs 13:4 says, *"The soul of the sluggard desireth, and hath nothing: but the soul of the diligent shall be made fat."* This verse says the sluggard has aspirations (desires) but has nothing. On the other hand, the diligent person has dreams and is *"made fat,"* which means *made successful.* Any person can set goals, but not just anyone will be diligent enough to reach them.

6. Diligence brings a reward from the Lord. Colossians 3:23 and 24 tells us, *"And whatsoever ye do, do it heartily, as to the Lord, and not unto men; Knowing that of the Lord ye shall receive the reward of the inheritance: for ye serve the Lord Christ."* It is encouraging to know that being diligent on Earth will bring rewards in Heaven. Every breath we take is an increase from God. If you are working hard for God (your Boss), you will be paid by Him. God rewards hard work. He does not always pay on the first or the fifteenth, but He always pays.

Three Characteristics of a Diligent Man

- **The diligent man does not waste food.** *"The slothful man roasteth not that which he took in hunting: but the substance of a diligent man is precious."* (Proverbs 12:27) The diligent person who earns his means does not waste the leftovers. In America, we throw more food away as scraps than most nations get to eat as their main course.
- **The diligent man is organized in his accounts.** Proverbs 27:23 says, *"Be thou diligent to know the state of thy flocks ...."* The diligent person keeps his checkbook balanced. His bills are in order and they are paid on time. He knows how much income is available and how much outgo is necessary. He does not hide from these figures, hoping they will go away.
- **The truly diligent man will use his diligence to do good.** Proverbs 11:27 says, *"He that diligently seeketh good procureth favour ...."* The Christian should be as diligent about doing good as the wicked are about doing bad. I would hate to think a wicked man cared more about evil than I did about good.

In conclusion, determine to be a diligent Christian. Lazy people envy the many rewards a diligent person enjoys. However, slothful people usually are not willing to pay the price to have the same rewards for themselves. Diligence is not an elusive dream that cannot be attained. Any person can learn to be diligent. All that is required is work.

Chapter 14

Character and Laziness

PROVERBS 21:25 AND 26 TEACHES, *"The desire of the slothful killeth him; for his hands refuse to labour. He coveteth greedily all the day long: but the righteous giveth and spareth not."* What is slothfulness? The word *sloth* means *lazy.* The word *slothful* means *full of sloth* or *laziness.*

Let's consider some of the inherent problems in America, the excuses the people make for having the problem when the real problem is slothfulness or laziness.

- Many people will not finish what they start.
- Many people do not have a job, even though there is not a shortage of employment opportunities.
- Many people will not live within their means; therefore, they depend on the government (welfare and food stamps) and blame their lack on the economy.
- Many people will grow fat and die from a heart attack and say heart disease is on the upswing.
- Many people will divorce after two years of marriage and place the blame on the immoral times in which we live.
- Many people will grow old and not have their needs and blame it on the fact that the social security system is failing.
- Many people will never own their own car or house and place the blame on inflation.

One word will address these excuses and the real reasons behind these problems — slothfulness or laziness.

Because of government programs today, we meet lazy people in all walks of life. Just drive around in a neighborhood and you can almost point at the homes where people live on welfare and food stamps. A large percentage of the homeless people on the street today are downright lazy. It is easier to walk to the post office and get a government handout than it is to work a job. I have yet to see a diligent Christian become a tramp.

The following are common symptoms I have observed in lazy people. Examine yourself. Having one symptom is placing your life in danger.

1. The lazy person does not think he is lazy. Proverbs 26:16 says, *"The sluggard is wiser in his own conceit than seven men that can render a reason."* Slothful people are always busy explaining why obstacles keep them from doing their work. The lazy person is always waiting for better working conditions; therefore, he will get the job done tomorrow.

Be careful of obeying statements like, "Don't work too hard." One reason our nation is falling apart is because of the labor unions striking for an honest day's pay. Pray tell me, what happened to an honest day's work?

Do you find yourself saying: "I can't find a job today; I'll get one tomorrow; I need a break"? One hundred times more people die due to laziness than die due to being overworked. If you are thinking right now that you are not slothful, you probably are. Will you admit you need character? If you make excuses about fulfilling duties in your Christian life, you are probably slothful.

2. The lazy person never gets a task finished. Proverbs 12:27 says, *"The slothful man roasteth not that which he took in hunting: but the substance of a diligent man is precious."* The Bible tells us that the hunter has fun on his hunt, but he won't clean the meat. To the slothful person, every job is a mountain of horror, not a door of opportunity. To the slothful person, school is a curse, not an opportunity to learn; he probably won't graduate. To the slothful person, working for parents is a curse, not an opportunity to prove his love to his parents.

Proverbs 24:30 and 31 says, *"I went by the field of the slothful, and by the vineyard of the man void of understanding; And, lo, it was all grown over with thorns, and nettles had covered the face thereof, and the stone wall thereof was broken down."* In these verses the Bible teaches us that the lazy person had a field, but he did not till the land. Therefore, the field was overgrown with weeds, a harvest was never brought in, and everything went to ruin. What a sad testimony!

3. The lazy person will always need a boss. Proverbs 12:24 teaches, *"The hand of the diligent shall bear rule: but the slothful shall be under tribute."* The sluggard is not a self-starter; he must have a boss to stand over him. The lazy man's philosophy is that nothing is so important that it cannot be done at another time. Today or now is not important to him. The slothful man never considers that he must give an account to God for his labor.

The slothful person perceives leaders as negative because they seem to recognize his laziness. (Rarely will a lazy man become a leader.) A trait of the slothful person is complaining. He gripes about inclement weather because it will ruin his playtime. However, the hard worker will find a way to work, even if it is raining.

Don't marry a lazy person. Don't hire a lazy person. To keep from hiring a lazy person, always seek character references. By all means, don't associate with a lazy person. Someone with character must oversee the characterless.

4. A lazy person will ignore the principles of his employer. Matthew 25:26-28 says, *"His lord answered and said unto him, Thou wicked and slothful servant, thou knewest that I reap where I sowed not, and gather where I have not strawed: Thou oughtest therefore to have put my money to the exchangers, and then at my coming I should have received mine own with usury. Take therefore the talent from him, and give it unto him which hath ten talents."* The servant in these verses was lazy. He would not invest the money entrusted to him in the way he knew his master would want him to invest it. The result was that the lazy person lost his opportunity to work with finances.

5. The lazy person is weak or soft. Proverbs 6:10 and 11 teaches, *"Yet a little sleep, a little slumber, a little folding of the hands to sleep: So shall thy poverty come as one that travelleth, and*

CHARACTER

thy want as an armed man." Usually a person becomes lazy gradually. Strong people start making many soft choices and start down the path to slothfulness. Needing just a little more rest or taking a few more minutes on break before starting the project or taking the easy road or doing the easy job takes a hard worker down the path to laziness.

Proverbs 20:4 says, *"The sluggard will not plow by reason of the cold; therefore shall he beg in harvest, and have nothing."* The lazy person says, "I can't go out and prepare the land for winter wheat. It's 45° F. I don't have a heated cab for my tractor. I will wait and plant corn in the spring." The slothful person says, "I don't want to dig ditches; I'm allergic to shovels"; or "I don't want to cut wood; I believe we must preserve the habitat for the spotted owl population." "I don't want to cut grass; I'm for leaving nature in its natural state." Before long, making excuses to cover laziness and choosing the easy way becomes a way of life — a soft, seemingly easy way.

6. The lazy person hurts those around him. Proverbs 18:9 says, *"He also that is slothful in his work is brother to him that is a great waster."* People who associate with a lazy man cannot depend on him. It is usually better to stay away from a lazy person. Many times when a shiftless person is given a job about which he complains, the boss sometimes tries to accommodate him by changing his work to suit him. However, it is not work that needs to be changed; the worker needs to change. Sometimes having this change will hurt the slothful person's feelings or self-esteem. Regardless of the hurt feelings, the lazy person soon starts making new excuses and finds reasons to back off from his new responsibility and pulls others down with his complaints.

Proverbs 10:26, *"As vinegar to the teeth, and as smoke to the eyes, so is the sluggard to them that send him."* Vinegar sets the teeth on edge; smoke makes the eyes water. That is exactly how the lazy person affects those around him. Slothful people care only about themselves, their wants, and their demands.

7. A lazy person is not known for his love of others. Romans 12:9-11 says, *"Let love be without dissimulation. Abhor that which is evil; cleave to that which is good. Be kindly affectioned one to another with brotherly love; in honour preferring one another; Not slothful in* *business; fervent in spirit; serving the Lord."* In the above Scripture, a description of the qualities of a person who loves others is given. If you truly love others, you will not be slothful in your treatment of them. As I stated before, lazy people care only for themselves. For a slothful person to care about others, he would have to stop thinking of himself.

8. A lazy person leads a life of discomfort. Proverbs 15:19 says, *"The way of the slothful man is as an hedge of thorns: but the way of the righteous is made plain."* A lazy person feels that to work is to be uncomfortable; however, a lazy person eventually discovers that **not** to work is usually **more** uncomfortable. By the time that discovery is made, it's too late for the lazy person to mend his ways. The slothful person does not have the knowledge or character to correct his plight.

9. The lazy only dream of success. Proverbs 21:25 and 26 teaches, *"The desire of the slothful killeth him; for his hands refuse to labour. He coveteth greedily all the day long: but the righteous giveth and spareth not."* Not working gives the lazy person time to dream of all the possessions he wants. Because of his big dreams and not working to fulfill them, he becomes depressed and cannot sleep.

Proverbs 26:14 verifies this: *"As the door turneth upon his hinges, so doth the slothful upon his bed."* All his unfulfilled dreams bring depression, no rest, and then no strength for work. He is so lazy that he even gets tired of dreaming and tired from being tired. Too much sleep makes you even more tired. Most dreams are nightmares to the lazy person, but a man of character will wake up and make the dream a reality.

10. The lazy person gives no thought for tomorrow. Proverbs 6:6 and 7 says, *"Go to the ant, thou sluggard; consider her ways, and be wise: Which having no guide, overseer, or ruler."* Lazy people have a I Corinthians 15:32 attitude: *"Let us eat and drink; for to morrow we die."* God made the ant with an instinct to prepare for the off-season. The sluggard does not even have the intelligence of an ant.

11. The lazy person will not take care of his house. Ecclesiastes 10:18 says, *"By much slothfulness the building decayeth; and through idleness of the hands the house droppeth through."* Do you fix broken

CHARACTER

items at home? Is your house in good repair? Do you keep the outside painted? Is the lawn nicely landscaped? Is the lawn manicured and trimmed?

Do you help to keep the house of God in good repair? When volunteer help is needed, do you offer your services?

12. The lazy person spends his time with people of like character. Proverbs 18:9 teaches, *"He also that is slothful in his work is brother to him that is a great waster."* The old saying, "Birds of a feather flock together," is true of lazy people. They attract and are attracted to lazy people and people who waste — time, food, and money.

Someone who wastes his food is someone who probably didn't have to earn it, or if he did earn it, he wasn't diligent in doing so. Because of that lack of diligence, he really has not paid full price for the money that bought the food, so he doesn't really appreciate it.

13. The lazy person believes his own lies and destroys himself. In Proverbs 22:13 we read, *"The slothful man saith, There is a lion without, I shall be slain in the streets."* The lazy person says, "I'm hungry," but he makes an excuse like, "It's too cold or too hot to work. I can't possibly earn the money to buy some food." He says, "A job will hurt me. There is a lion without." He has lied to himself about his laziness for so long that he now believes his lies and destroys himself. The age-old adage is true: "A little hard work never killed anyone."

In today's society, often a little injury gives people the excuse to be placed on the disabled list for the rest of their lives. These lazy people convince themselves that to work is to destroy themselves.

Characterless people are not concerned with keeping a good work record. They don't mind even lying to themselves and making excuses for not working. How sad to live a life of laziness!

These 13 points encompass the problems of many people in America today.

Chapter 15

Character
and
Our Need to Be Accountable

LUKE 15:11-24 SAYS, *"And he said, a certain man had two sons: And the younger of them said to his father, Father, give me the portion of goods that falleth to me. And he divided unto them his living. And not many days after the younger son gathered all together, and took his journey into a far country, and there wasted his substance with riotous living. And when he had spent all, there arose a mighty famine in that land; and he began to be in want. And he went and joined himself to a citizen of that country; and he sent him into his fields to feed swine. And he would fain have filled his belly with the husks that the swine did eat: and no man gave unto him. And when he came to himself, he said, How many hired servants of my father's have bread enough and to spare, and I perish with hunger! I will arise and go to my father, and will say unto him, Father, I have sinned against heaven, and before thee, And am no more worthy to be called thy son: make me as one of thy hired servants. And he arose, and came to his father. But when he was yet a great way off, his father saw him, and had compassion, and ran, and fell on his neck, and kissed him. And the son said unto him, Father, I have sinned against heaven, and in thy sight, and am no more worthy to be called thy son. But the father said to his servants, Bring forth the best robe, and put it on him; and put a ring on his hand, and shoes on his feet: And bring hither the fatted calf, and kill it; and let us eat, and be merry: For this my son was dead, and is alive again; he was lost, and*

CHARACTER

is found. And they began to be merry."

These verses give the very famous account of the prodigal son. We can surely surmise from what the Bible says that this young man had a brother and a dad who was probably a businessman. We know that he had many servants. The prodigal came to his father and wanted all the money that he had coming to him so he could leave home. His father gave him his share. I have no doubt that young man walked away from home with a pocketful of money thinking he had it made. He now had his freedom.

The Bible teaches in this story that the prodigal found it is more expensive to live in the world than he thought. Part of the reason may have been the fact that there was a famine. Before long he had spent all of his inheritance. In order to live, he had to take a job feeding hogs. The Bible says he even thought about eating what the hogs were eating because he was so hungry, and no one would help him. No doubt, his plight made him think of home and what he left behind.

The prodigal decided that going home and working as a servant would be better than living with the hogs. I believe this prodigal prepared many dialogues on his way home from the far country. I'm sure he wondered if he would be accepted again in his home.

Little did the prodigal know that every night his dad went out on the front porch to watch the road, just hoping his boy would come home. Sure enough, the prodigal's father was out watching the road that night. In fact, the Bible says the father saw the boy coming and ran to him with open arms. The boy said to his father that he didn't deserve his father's name and home. The prodigal asked to serve his father as hired help.

It would surely seem this young man probably learned quite a few lessons while feeding hogs in a far country. Let me share some principles I have learned about being accountable.

1. In your youth, you need to be accountable to someone. Luke 15:12 says, *"And the younger of them said to his father, Father, give me the portion of goods that falleth to me. And he divided unto them his living."* I believe the prodigal left home before he was ready. He was the **younger** of the two brothers. Perhaps his older brother was wise enough to realize that he was not ready to go out into the world. This teaches that the **older** brother did not begin to feel that his training was complete.

Every Christian needs to be trained at church to do what is right. Don't ever leave the training station. Just say, "I'm going to be in church every time the church doors are open." You are never wise enough to go without church. Dr. Lee Roberson is famous for a statement: "It takes three to thrive — Sunday morning, Sunday night, and Wednesday night." Do not miss church.

Do not quit high school and college. You are not ready for the world yet. If you do quit school, just make sure that you don't go on welfare so I have to support you. The prodigal son left home before he was trained to be what he needed to be away from home. You need to be accountable to someone in your youth if you plan to be a success.

2. Face yourself concerning your need to be accountable. Luke 15:17 tells us, *"And when he came to himself, he said, How many hired servants of my father's have bread enough and to spare ...."* Thank God the prodigal came to himself! In other words, he realized that he left before he was trained completely. If you have left the church, and if you have left home and quit school (and if you are truthful), you are not succeeding, and you know it.

The prodigal realized he had no character. Face the facts: you need to be accountable to someone who will help you to develop your character. Do you know the importance of being on time? When you don't show up on time, you are sinning against the people waiting for you — you are wasting their time. It is nobody else's fault but your own that you are not punctual. Are you where you are supposed to be on time? Do you keep your word? Are you trustworthy? Do you finish what you start?

3. You need to ask someone to "please make you" into a person with character. Luke 15:19b says, *"Make me as one of thy hired servants."* The prodigal boy realized he needed help and asked his father to let him be a servant. What he was saying was, "Make me do what is right." If I could read between the lines, I believe he was saying, "I don't deserve the privileges of being a son. I need to be like a servant. I need to go live in the servants' quarters. I want you to teach me and to make me do right because I can't make myself do right."

If you are struggling with having character in your life, you need to get to somebody who has character and say, "Please, help me learn to do right." I personally search for people in my life who will make me do right. There is a simple reason why you don't do right — you don't have the character to do right. Find somebody who can **make you do right.** You need to go to a Christian school where leaders will **make** you do right! You need your parents to **make** you do right. If you don't have the character to do right, find somebody who will **make** you do it.

4. Everybody at least has the character to become accountable to someone. You need to learn to submit to a power that will help you become what you need to become. You need to learn to submit to the Holy Spirit's power, which will make you become what you need to become. Submit to what God is showing you from the Bible. You may be lacking in character, but you are not helpless. Get to someone for aid.

When my girlfriend and I were dating, we never dated alone. Would you like to know the reason why? It was because I wanted to touch her. However, I knew the Bible teaches that I was not to touch her until we were married. Therefore, I had a chaperon that went with us everywhere. The reason I had that chaperon in the car for every date was so that I was accountable to him to do right.

There was a time in America that when a young man joined the armed services he was, in essence, saying, "Please make me into a man."

5. Once you have learned to be accountable, stay with it until your leaders say you are properly trained. Don't depend on your own opinion. Still seek counsel when you need help.

6. Please accept the fact that we are all going to be accountable to someone forever. We will be under the direction of God and His Word for all eternity. He is trying to develop the character of Christ in us.

Chapter 16

Character and When Our Flesh Is Weak

THE BIBLE SAYS IN Matthew 26:41, *"Watch and pray, that ye enter not into temptation: the spirit indeed is willing, but the flesh is weak."* When we were saved, the Bible teaches that the Spirit of God moved in and now lives inside of us. In I Corinthians 6:19 the Bible says, *"What? know ye not that your body is the temple of the Holy Ghost, which is in you, which ye have of God, and ye are not your own?"* That means that within me right now, because I am saved, resides the Holy Spirit of God. The Bible also tells me in Matthew 26:41 that His Spirit within me is willing. The question is, what is that Spirit willing to do? He is willing to do right. What is "right"? "Right" is whatever the Bible says because the Spirit of God always has us do right according to the Bible.

If you are saved today, within you is that very same Spirit of God. I have the same Spirit of God in me that John the Baptist had dwelling in him. I have the same Spirit of God in me that Paul had dwelling in him.

An old missionary had gone to a tribe of Indians and had won an Indian to Christ. One day the Indian was talking with the missionary and said, "Missionary, it is hard. It is hard to live for Christ. I realize I have Christ in me, but it is still so hard." The Indian convert began to explain to the missionary in the best way he knew how what was taking place. "Inside me lives white dog, and also inside me lives black dog. Black dog is the old me who wants to do bad things. White dog is the Spirit of God — He wants to do God's things. The white dog and the black dog — they fight all the time. White dog want to do right; black dog want to do wrong."

The missionary said, "Well, who usually wins the fight — the white dog or the black dog?" The old Indian answered, "Whichever one me feed most."

Within you lives the Spirit of God Who wants you to do right, but also there is that old nature in you which we call the flesh — the black dog, if you please. That old nature wants you to do wrong. The nature you feed the most is going to be victorious.

Are you feeding the Spirit of God or are you doing that which would strengthen the flesh? In order to feed the proper nature, we need to be aware of times when it might be easier to feed the "black dog." The Bible tells us there are times when we will be weak. Our character level should cause us to avoid these times so we can be victorious in our Christian life.

1. We are weak at night. Proverbs 7:7-12 says, *"And beheld among the simple ones, I discerned among the youths, a young man void of understanding, Passing through the street near her corner; and he went the way to her house, In the twilight, in the evening, in the black and dark night: And, behold, there met him a woman with the attire of an harlot, and subtil of heart. (She is loud and stubborn; her feet abide not in her house: Now is she without, now in the streets, and lieth in wait at every corner.)"* It was dark, and it was a late hour. A young man passing through a certain block in his city met a wicked woman who wore the attire of a harlot. The Bible lists many characteristics of this woman. She was loud. She was subtil — clever and sly. She was dressed in a wicked, seductive way. Proverbs 7:21 and 22 says, *"With her much fair speech she caused him to yield, with the flattering of her lips she forced him. He goeth after her straightway, as an ox goeth to the slaughter, or as a fool to the correction of the stocks."* The young man committed a terrible sin, perhaps thinking no one would see him during the late hours.

John 3:19 says, *"And this is the condemnation, that light is come into the world, and men loved darkness rather than light, because their deeds were evil."* I believe we are weakest when it is dark.

CHARACTER AND WHEN OUR FLESH IS WEAK

Remember, the spirit indeed is willing, but the flesh is weak. The nighttime hours have always held certain enticements. A big time at the bar is the late evening hours. The big time for the dance is during the evening hours. Robbery, murder, and violent crimes usually take place during the evening hours when unseen. Probably 95 percent of the incidences of immorality are committed at nighttime. Why? Because there is something about darkness, the night, and the midnight hour that the Devil enjoys using. John 3:19 says that Jesus came into the world and was the Light of the world. Get in the light! Stay in the light! We know that evil lurks in the darkness. Therefore, we must realize that the evening hours is one of the times when we are weakest.

2. We are weak when we get out of our schedule. II Samuel 11:1 says, *"And it came to pass, after the year was expired, at the time when kings go forth to battle, that David sent Joab, and his servants with him, and all Israel; and they destroyed the children of Ammon, and besieged Rabbah. But David tarried still at Jerusalem."*

As leader of the forces, David should have gone to battle with his men, but David chose to tarry at Jerusalem. In other words, David got out of his usual routine. Because he was home, he saw Bath-sheba bathing on the roof of her home. Because of her beauty, David lusted after her and called her to come to his home, where he committed immorality and eventually tried to cover his sin by having her husband killed. Allow me to explain why all that happened. Quite simply, David wasn't **where** he was supposed to be **when** he was supposed to be there. *"The spirit indeed is willing, but the flesh is weak."* The Bible says it was a time for kings to be in battle; David set himself up for a time of weakness.

When you get out of schedule — watch out! The Devil knows it is a time he can attack. Teens cause more problems on the weekend than they do during the week. Why? During the week they are scheduled; they get up at the same time and spend the day at school. There the people in authority tell them when to sit, when to walk, when to talk, when to close the door, and when to eat. A schedule has been created; but once teens get out of schedule, they are apt to get in trouble. Because teens usually have no schedule in the evening, they

CHARACTER

probably sin more at night than they do during the day at school.

Be careful during your weekends. More people get away from God on the weekend than they do during the week. Keep yourself on schedule during the weekends. Vacation times are also times when great care should be exercised to try and establish some semblance of a schedule. Get up at the same time as usual. Spend the same amount of time with God. As much as possible, eat at the usual time. Remember, we are weak when we get out of our routine.

3. We are weak when hungry. Matthew 4:1-4 says, *"Then was Jesus led up of the spirit into the wilderness to be tempted of the devil. And when he had fasted forty days and forty nights, he was afterward an hungred. And when the tempter came to him, he said, If thou be the Son of God, command that these stones be made bread. But he answered and said, It is written, Man shall not live by bread alone, but by every word that proceedeth out of the mouth of God."* The Bible says in Matthew 4 that Jesus had been fasting and praying. The Devil knew Jesus was hungry so he told Jesus to turn the stones into food. But Jesus said, *"Man shall not live by bread alone, but by every word that proceedeth out of the mouth of God."* The Devil came to tempt Him because Jesus was physically weak because of hunger.

In Genesis 25 the Bible gives another example of the weakness that can be caused by hunger. Esau, the firstborn son of Isaac and Rebekah, had been out hunting. He arrived home tired and hungry — so hungry he believed he would die. Jacob happened to be cooking, and Esau said, *"Feed me, I pray thee, with that same red pottage; for I am faint."* (Genesis 25:30) Jacob said, *"Sell me this day thy birthright."* The Bible says Esau despised his birthright, and he sold it to Jacob for bread and lentils.

The two examples show that when you are hungry, it causes weakness of the flesh. These two illustrations both talk about physical food. However, people can be hungry for more than just food. There are other appetites some people crave to be fulfilled. Be careful that you do not allow your appetites to run wild. For instance, seeking money or fame can also cause weakness.

I coach soccer. I find one of the biggest problems I have with my junior high soccer team is to get the boys to stop thinking about girls.

In the same way, I can't get the girls to stop thinking about anything but boys. Recently, I was on the soccer bus, and I needed to coach my soccer players about being ready to play the toughest team we would play all year. I had to say, "You guys have got to get your mind off the girls! There are more important things at this moment than a girl!" I almost had to set off a bomb in the bus to get their eyes and mind off those girls!

A man's uncurbed appetite for a woman will cause his flesh to be weak, and the Spirit may never dominate his life. We must learn to control ourselves. Young ladies need to learn to control their appetites for members of the opposite sex also. Get your appetites under control. Learning and attaining character means gaining and keeping control of your appetites.

4. We are weak when tired. I Kings 19:4 says, *"But he himself went a day's journey into the wilderness, and came and sat down under a juniper tree: and he requested for himself that he might die; and said, It is enough; now, O LORD, take away my life; for I am not better than my fathers."* Elijah had confronted more than 400 prophets of Baal on Mount Carmel. He had called down fire from Heaven, which totally consumed a sacrifice that had been water drenched. He had single-handedly slaughtered over 400 men. When Jezebel heard of Elijah's victory and how he had killed her false prophets, in so many words she said, "I'm going to get him." The result: Elijah ran from her. I believe he ran because he was dead tired.

One principle we can learn from the life of Elijah is to get the proper amount of sleep. Christians must learn to take care of themselves. Why? Many people who make irresponsible mistakes with their lives do so because they are too tired to make right decisions. Everyone must have the proper amount of sleep to function well. Becoming too exhausted to listen in church will lend toward making more mistakes.

Recently a young businessman came to me and said, "Brother Owens, I just got a contract for $15,000.00! I will make $15,000.00 in one week. I have to put in a lot of hours."

I said to him, "You should never work so hard in and for the world that all your energy is gone and you cannot work for God."

CHARACTER

He said, "But I'm going to do good!"

Yes, more than likely he would do good with his money, but the only problem was that he was going to be so tired at the end of the week that he would probably sleep during Sunday school and church. If he does manage to stay awake, his mind will be too tired to grasp the truths from the preaching. *Never get so tired that you cannot do right.*

5. We are weak when we cease to be obedient in the area of the Great Commission. Matthew 28:19 and 20 says, *"Go ye therefore, and teach all nations, baptizing them in the name of the Father, and of the Son, and of the Holy Ghost: Teaching them to observe all things whatsoever I have commanded you: and, lo, I am with you alway, even unto the end of the world. Amen."* If, at one time, you have been a soul winner, and you have stopped going soul winning, no doubt you have become very weak. One purpose for the Holy Spirit being given to us is for winning souls.

6. Married people are weak when away from their spouse too much. I Corinthians 7:5 teaches, *"Defraud ye not one the other, except it be with consent for a time, that ye may give yourselves to fasting and prayer; and come together again, that Satan tempt you not for your incontinency."* A married person who is away from his spouse in the area of intimacy is tempted easily. A husband and wife need to come together physically to remain strong in this area. A good evangelist realizes this and does not let the Devil catch him off guard when he is weak. It may be a good idea for someone who travels to take his spouse along from time to time.

Every person must learn to recognize the times when he is weak. During those times, the person must do whatever he can to correct the situation. If hungry, eat. If unscheduled, purchase a schedule book and make a schedule. Because we have the Holy Spirit living within us, we have the wherewithal to combat effectively the times of weakness we encounter.

Chapter 17

Character
and
Developing It in Our Children

PROVERBS 6:6-11 SAYS, *"Go to the ant, thou sluggard; consider her ways, and be wise: Which having no guide, overseer, or ruler, Provideth her meat in the summer, and gathereth her food in the harvest. How long wilt thou sleep, O sluggard? when wilt thou arise out of thy sleep? Yet a little sleep, a little slumber, a little folding of the hands to sleep: So shall thy poverty come as one that travelleth, and thy want as an armed man."*

Proverbs 22:6 commands us to *"Train up a child in the way he should go: and when he is old, he will not depart from it."* If we do not train our children to work, we are training them not to work. If we do not help our children develop character, we are helping them to have no character. The best time to help a child with his character is in his early years. There are many reasons for this. The following are but a few:

- Children spend much time with their parents.
- Children have a great desire to learn.
- Children are still moldable in attitude.
- Children have great faith in their parents.
- Children will consider the training fun if approached correctly.

I find the old adage, "You can't teach an old dog new tricks," is very nearly true. Because I find this saying true, allow me to share some thoughts on how to teach character to children.

CHARACTER

1. A child needs an example of character, not just an instructor. Young people do not always listen to their parents, but they rarely fail to imitate them.

2. A child needs help with his work attitude. Teach children that work is a reward, not a punishment. If children perceive work as punishment, someday they probably won't want a job. Teach them work is fulfilling. Little girls should enjoy playing house and learn to cook, sew, iron, and clean. Little boys should have play tools and play lawn mowers. My preacher, Brother Hyles, often uses an illustration of how his son Dave had a play lawn mower, and Dave would copy his dad mowing the lawn. Brother Hyles goes on to say that when Dave became a teenager, they exchanged lawn mowers! What an excellent way to teach a child that work is fun and rewarding.

3. A child could work for his toys. If a child sees toys that he wants, set up some type of system where he or she could earn that toy. Make a chart to show where hours or tasks are logged and rewarded. Do not just give children all for which they ask.

4. A child could be taught to make toys. Teach them to create their own fun. How many times at Christmas have you seen children enjoying the boxes instead of the toys? This also teaches creativity and a sense of accomplishment.

5. A child should have responsibility in the house. The Bible teaches in II Thessalonians 3:10 that you do not eat if you will not work. *"For even when we were with you, this we commanded you, that if any would not work, neither should he eat."* The Bible plainly teaches that if someone will not work, he should not eat! Have children do a certain amount of work and explain to them they are earning some of their benefits. Following this verse could help do away with the welfare philosophy.

6. A child needs to learn teamwork by a family example. A child needs to learn that if he does not help the family, he will hurt the family. Anyone who does not do his part hurts the whole unit. For example, work in the yard together or on cleaning the house as a team. Every person, young and old alike, must learn to function in the church and society in this way. Playing sports together will help develop a team spirit as well.

7. A child must be taught to do all his assigned chores correctly the first time. Time is life. When work has to be done over and over again, time is wasted; therefore, much of life is wasted by redoing work.

8. A child needs to be trained to finish the job. *"And Jesus said unto him, No man, having put his hand to the plough, and looking back, is fit for the kingdom of God."* (Luke 9:62) Finishing the job means not looking back. Just learning this concept will help a young person to stand head and shoulders above most adults.

9. A child needs to understand that "work" and "labor" are good words. More days off than on will cause a worker to become lazy and unproductive. If a child must get dirty to work, it is acceptable and necessary. Getting dirty will especially help a boy from being a sissy. Mothers, let your boys get dirty.

10. A child should choose hobbies that are constructive. Allow a child to compose stories and poems and to make a book of his thoughts. Be sure a child has toys that nurture creativity like Legos, Lincoln Logs, blocks, and ice-cream sticks. A child ought to observe nature. The Bible gives many character lessons using animals as illustrations. For instance, Isaiah 40:31 teaches to be strong like an eagle. God even uses the insect world to illustrate character. Proverbs 6:6 teaches about the ant and its labor. Let your child have an ant farm. I believe the Bible teaches he will learn by observing how to have character.

11. A child needs to be taught to choose an occupation that will serve mankind. Working in full-time Christian service as a preacher, assistant pastor, Christian school teacher, or as a doctor, plumber, carpenter are all occupations that serve mankind. Having a goal to become a great basketball or football player is having a goal of being exactly that: A PLAYER. Don't play all your life.

12. A child needs to be trained to obey so he can obey his leaders someday. Of course, ultimately his obedience development is for serving God.

13. A child needs, at first, to be trained to work with an on-site supervisor. That first on-site supervisor ought to be the child's mom or dad.

CHARACTER

14. A child needs to be trained to work even when the boss can't see him. If a child can learn this, he probably will become the boss someday. It is rare to find an employer who can trust his employees. Teach children that God is always watching, even when their human boss is not. *"The eyes of the LORD are in every place, beholding the evil and the good."* (Proverbs 15:3)

15. Teach a child that he does not have to be intellectually-minded to be a success. To be a success, a child must learn to work. He must carry that work ethic on through the teenage years and adulthood. Work is the key to developing a good mind.

16. Teach children how to plan their work. It is good to write down assigned tasks and duties to be performed in a certain amount of time. The list should be organized and in order of importance. Always be organized and set priorities in order.

17. A child needs to be taught that hard work will keep his body healthy. It seems we have more sickness in our society today than ever. Could we assume this fact might be because we have more characterless people as well?

18. A child needs to be taught that hard work will help him sleep better. Most insomniacs are not ditch diggers. A hard worker usually sleeps well. He sleeps with a sense of fulfillment.

19. A child needs to be taught that hard workers appreciate their food more than a lazy person. I believe that I enjoy my oatmeal more than food stamp recipients enjoy their steak because I **earned** my oatmeal.

We have a characterless generation of young people. This is a direct result of a characterless generation of parents. This vicious cycle must stop with you. Some parents may want to memorize and start practicing these principles for themselves. The epigram is still true: "A little hard work never killed anyone."

Chapter 18

Character
and
Respect for Our Elders

PSALM 37:25 SAYS, *"I have been young, and now am old; yet have I not seen the righteous forsaken, nor his seed begging bread."* David is saying that he once was young and now is old. Time passes so quickly; all too soon the youth will become the aged ones. The older you get, the more aware you become of how few hours you actually have left. However, the opposite is true of youth.

You can say to a child, "It is going to be about an hour before we leave. Go play." Typically, that child will come back in two minutes and ask, "Is it time to go yet?" An hour seems like a very, very long time to children. When you are young, time is measured in minutes. When you reach adolescence, time is measured in hours. When you become a young adult, time is measured in days, weeks, months, years, and then in decades. When you become a senior citizen, time is once again measured in minutes and hours.

Do you realize how quickly time passes? *"Whereas ye know not what shall be on the morrow. For what is your life? It is even a vapour, that appeareth for a little time, and then vanisheth away."* (James 4:14) Because time passes so quickly, I felt a chapter on the treatment of the aged was essential to this book. I hope you get to reap what you have sown concerning this topic. Let me ask you a question: Would you want to be treated by someone someday the same way you treat your elders?

A nation of people which respects their aged will stay a strong nation. I believe one of the reasons why America is falling apart today is a direct result of improper treatment of our aged. The eastern countries are recognized as being nations of strength. Why? As a general rule, the youth respect their elders. Unfortunately, this characteristic is not taught to young people in America today.

The American people are making some drastic errors in the treatment of the elderly. There are corporations all over this great nation who have decided to get rid of the old man because he seems to be slowing down progress. The corporate owners want to force the elderly into retirement. This is a mistake. New employees need to learn from the experience and wisdom of retirement-age people.

There are people who eagerly await their parents' or grandparents' deaths for an inheritance because they don't want to work; or they break the loved ones' hearts by trying to nullify a will or trust to receive the inheritance they feel is due them. America has forgotten her aged. There are many elderly people who need someone to love them for themselves. These forgotten ones are everywhere. I have learned some of the most wonderful lessons of life while fellowshipping with lonely people in nursing homes.

The following are some Biblical principles regarding treatment of the elderly:

1. The youth ought to stand to their feet in the presence of older people. Leviticus 19:32a commands, *"Thou shalt rise up before the hoary head."* You say, "I thought that custom was just in some antiquated etiquette book?" It is! The Bible is an etiquette book. There was a day that when an elder entered the room, youth automatically stood. Sad to say, that kind of respect is missing in America today. There was a time in America that if a teacher entered the classroom, the students stood out of respect. There was a time when children used to stand in the presence of their parents and grandparents. There was also a time in America when the youth gave their seats to the ladies and the elderly. Rare is the instance when you will see this kind of respect shown today.

2. We are to honor the older people. Leviticus 19:32 charges, *"Thou shalt rise up before the hoary head, and honour the face of the old man, and fear thy God: I am the LORD."* When the Bible uses the word *"honor"* in this verse, it means that we are to treat the aged as a possession that is precious. Something treated with honor is something of great value. Our elders are of great value and ought to be treated as such. Deuteronomy 5:16a says, *"Honour thy father and thy mother."* Exodus 20:12 says, *"Honour thy father and thy mother: that thy days may be long upon the land which the LORD thy God giveth thee."* The Bible teaches that if you honor your parents, you will receive a benefit — longer life! Quite simply, old age is a result of honoring old age. A person who esteems the hoary head becomes the honored one. Older people always feel honored when the youth choose to spend time with them.

I often wonder where the great men of conviction are for the next generation. I can promise you this: They are not frolicking among their peers. The reason we have a Dr. Jack Hyles is because Jack Hyles didn't spend his time with people his own age. He sought out and learned from senior citizens who had the wisdom that he needed to become a great man for his generation. In his preaching, Dr. Hyles often tells of how, as a young man, he invited patriarchs of the faith to fill his pulpit in order to learn from them.

Do you spend all your time with people your own age? It is sad, but true, that most young people have no concept about how to treat older people. We need to get the youth back to once again honoring mom and dad, grandma and grandpa and respecting the seasoned people who built our country and our churches.

Spend time with some of the old people who believe the old way, who act the old way, and who preach the old way. Learn some of the precepts and principles of the aged people. One of the best ways to get character is to spend time with someone who is a person of character.

3. We are to see the real beauty in older people. Proverbs 20:29 teaches, *"The glory of young men is their strength: and the beauty of old men is the grey head."* Do you know that the Bible says that gray hair is the beauty of an old man? Many people try to conceal what God says is their beauty! God says beauty is in wrinkles. All too often, people don't understand what true beauty is. There are some older people with gray hair and wrinkled faces who are very, very beautiful. The Bible says that we ought to see and recognize the

CHARACTER

beauty of old age. The beauty of wisdom is an inner beauty. Your life will become beautiful if you learn some lessons from your elders. No matter how old you are, there is someone from whom you can learn.

4. We are to see the royalty of older people. Proverbs 16:31a says, *"The hoary head is a crown of glory."* Typically today, a crown is reserved for royalty — for kings and queens to display. We do not just honor the elderly because they are older; they are to be honored as royal people. It is scriptural and right to ennoble and to venerate the older people. Buy your father a nice reclining chair and tell him that it is a throne.

We have heard Brother Hyles give the illustration of how, as a young boy, he used to look at his careworn, exhausted mother and think, "Someday I am going to make my mother into a queen." After Brother Hyles became a successful pastor, his mother sat about four or five rows back in the center section of the First Baptist Church of Hammond. One day he saw her gray hair and realized, "I have done everything I could to make Mother a queen, but she's already a queen. There she sits with her crown."

Young people, you need to realize that your parents are royalty. Your mom is a queen and ought to be treated as such. Your dad is a king and ought to be treated as such. Your grandparents ought to be treated as royalty. Ask yourself: Do I give my parents and grandparents the honor and the dignity that they deserve?

In 1989 my wife had the privilege of hostessing Mrs. John R. Rice at the last Christian Womanhood Ladies Spectacular that Mrs. Rice attended. Mrs. Marlene Evans, the founder and editor of the *Christian Womanhood* paper and leader of the Spectacular, had asked Schery to be Mrs. Rice's escort for the week. I cannot tell you how much this opportunity meant to my wife. Mrs. Rice's hairdresser was unable to be with her that week. Because Schery is a cosmetologist, she got to do Mrs. Rice's hair. Pictures were made of Schery helping Mrs. Rice. Schery picked up Mrs. Rice at her motel, escorted her throughout the day, ate meals with her, and returned her to the motel at the end of the day.

One of the days while Schery and Mrs. Rice were traveling to the church, Mrs. Rice looked out the window and saw an advertisement for alcoholic beverages on a billboard. My wife told how Mrs. Rice turned to her, almost frantic, and said, "Oh, Honey, please teach your children to hate sin, or they will try it." Since that day, we have been teaching our three boys and one daughter not to be pacifists but to hate sin. I believe the words of the matriarch: "If you don't teach them to hate sin, they will try it." The time Schery spent with a sweet, over 90-year-old lady may have salvaged my children.

Unfortunately, most young people do not want to be bothered with a gray-haired, slow, older person. In America today, the youth are always in a hurry, and they want to get the old people off the road. What an appalling testimony to our heritage! Most older folks are deemed to be a bother in today's society, and that's a sad situation. We are trying to take them off the roads constructed by their hard work, and the young generation doesn't have the sense to see they travel on roads constructed by the character of their elders.

5. We are to care for older people and meet their needs. Ruth 4:15 says, *"And he shall be unto thee a restorer of thy life, and a nourisher of thine old age: for thy daughter in law, which loveth thee, which is better to thee than seven sons, hath born him."* The story of Ruth and Naomi is one of the most well-known stories in the Bible. Naomi and her family left Beth-lehem-judah to sojourn in Moab. However, the family sojourned long enough for Naomi's husband Elimelech to die, for her two sons to marry, and then for both of the sons to die. Naomi returned to Beth-lehem-judah a bitter woman. The only family remaining with her was her daughter-in-law, Ruth. Naomi said to her former neighbors in Ruth 1:21a, *"I went out full, and the LORD brought me home again empty."* Of course, the hand of God is evident in these losses because Naomi guided Ruth into a beautiful marriage with Boaz. God gave Boaz and Ruth a son destined to be a famous man in Israel. Naomi became Obed's nurse, and God gave her a child to nourish her in her old age.

From this beautiful story of Naomi and Ruth, we ought to learn the principle of being a need-filler for elderly people. There are many ways young people can easily serve the elderly: cut their lawns in the summer and shovel their snow in the winter; provide transportation to the doctor, grocery store, or church for elderly people; be company for them on lonely evenings; ask questions and listen to them.

I Timothy 5:1-3, 8 says, *"Rebuke not an elder, but intreat him as a father; and the younger men as brethren; The elder women as mothers; the younger as sisters, with all purity. Honour widows that are widows indeed. But if any provide not for his own, and specially for those of his own house, he hath denied the faith, and is worse than an infidel."* These verses speak of taking care of the old. The Bible plainly states that those who do not care for the elderly are worse than unbelievers. A church should also help care for the older, especially the *"widows indeed,"* who are widows without any living relatives. Welfare for the elderly would be unheard of if the youth cared for the elderly.

At the top of your list of people for whom you should care ought to be your parents. Their needs should be met first. They should not have to live with the fear of being placed in a nursing home. If possible, prepare your home in such a way as to let them live with you when they can no longer care for themselves. You might think if you do that, your standard of living would go down. Perhaps two children would have to share a room. The grocery bills would be higher. Extra medical bills would be involved. It may mean having roles reversed to the point where you feel as if you had a baby again — only a fully-grown baby. All this may be true. I believe you owe this to those who did all this (and probably more) for you when you were a child. Our characterless generation receives life from our parents, but our lack of character makes us unwilling to repay them for their sacrifices on our behalf.

6. Special care should be given to remember your grandparents. The Bible says in II Timothy 1:5 and 6, *"When I call to remembrance the unfeigned faith that is in thee, which dwelt first in thy grandmother Lois, and thy mother Eunice; and I am persuaded that in thee also. Wherefore I put thee in remembrance that thou stir up the gift of God, which is in thee by the putting on of my hands."* In these verses Paul attributes Timothy's faith to the careful rearing of his mother Eunice and his grandmother Lois. I believe God wants us to remember and revere our grandparents. We ought to call them on the phone or write them regularly. Send cards and flowers on special occasions. Never forget their birthdays or anniversary or Christmas. Take a gift by their home. Many people do more for their pets, cars, and plants than for their grandparents. Always remember, your grandparents gave you your parents.

7. Follow the counsel of older people. I Kings 12:13 says, *"And the king answered the people roughly, and forsook the old men's counsel that they gave him."* Rehoboam was a young king who sought counsel from the young and the old, but he chose to take the advice of the youth. Because of this decision, his kingdom was divided. From this account we learn that we should seek and heed the advice of older, more spiritual people. We can learn from their mistakes. Someone has said that experience is not the best teacher — someone else's experience is. In essence we could bypass in our lives the errors they made. Older people will perceive you as wise for asking them questions.

The youth say, "I want to be heard." Their speech begs, "Someone look at **me**; pay attention to **me**." Youth can be heard, but youth must learn first. Most of them have nothing worth hearing. The elderly often have plenty to say, but no one wants to listen. Older people feel the same way as the youth about not being heard, but they **do** have something to say worthy of our attention.

There is a reward for showing respect for your elders. **Respect for your elders will lengthen your life.** Proverbs 4:7-10 tells us, *"Wisdom is the principal thing; therefore get wisdom: and with all thy getting get understanding. Exalt her, and she shall promote thee: she shall bring thee to honour, when thou dost embrace her. She shall give to thine head an ornament of grace: a crown of glory shall she deliver to thee. Hear, O my son, and receive my sayings; and the years of thy life shall be many."* If you want to live a long life, seek wisdom. God promises you that you can live longer if you have wisdom.

Proverbs 16:31 says, *"The hoary head is a crown of glory, if it be found in the way of righteousness."* This verse is speaking about the "gray hair" which marks the older generation. Proverbs 20:29, *"The glory of young men is their strength: and the beauty of old men is the grey head."* God is plainly saying in these verses that if you want to

CHARACTER

live a long time, you need to seek wisdom. The Bible very clearly teaches that the ones possessing wisdom are those who have gray hair. God is offering long life to us! All these verses teach that seeking and gaining wisdom will help you to live longer, and one way you can obtain wisdom is from older people.

Proverbs 13:20 says, *"He that walketh with wise men shall be wise: but a companion of fools shall be destroyed."* You will find that the wisest people on the face of this earth are usually the oldest people. That gray hair is a result of years of learning. ***Having proper respect for your elders will help you to become like them — wise.***

See to the needs of your grandparents and parents; ask them to tell you stories of their youth. Look at their photographs. Seek out the older people sitting alone at church; befriend them. Be an oft-seen visitor at nursing homes. The young people of our characterless generation need to go toward the elders who have been champions of character. If we do not, our own children's futures will be destroyed.

Chapter 19

Character and Having the Sense to Avoid What You Cannot Resist

BECAUSE JOSEPH WAS THE beloved son of his father, Jacob, his brothers were very jealous of him. At one point when his brothers were plotting to kill him, Reuben intervened and convinced them to spare Joseph's life. *"And Reuben said unto them, Shed no blood, but cast him into this pit that is in the wilderness, and lay no hand upon him; that he might rid him out of their hands, to deliver him to his father again."* (Genesis 37:22) Reuben even contemplated returning an unharmed Joseph to Jacob. The Bible does not say why, but Reuben left for a while.

After putting Joseph in the pit, the brothers saw a caravan of Ishmeelites passing through on their way to Egypt. Judah, one of the older brothers, decided to sell Joseph and make money rather than kill him. So rather than have Joseph's blood on their hands, they sold him for 20 pieces of silver.

Reuben returned to find that his brothers had sold Joseph. The Bible says, *"And Reuben returned unto the pit; and, behold, Joseph was not in the pit; and he rent his clothes."* (Genesis 37:29) To hide their complicity, the brothers then took Joseph's coat, tore it in pieces, dipped it in goat's blood, and carried it back to Jacob saying, *"This have we found: know now whether it be thy son's coat or no."* (Genesis 37:32b) Jacob assumed that Joseph had been torn to pieces by a wild animal.

When the Ishmeelite caravan reached Egypt, Joseph was sold to

CHARACTER

Potiphar, an officer of Pharaoh. Potiphar saw that *"... the LORD was with Joseph."* (Genesis 39:2a) Everything Joseph touched prospered. Potiphar soon gave Joseph a promotion and made him overseer of the "Potiphar estate." The Bible says in Genesis 39:5, *"... that the LORD blessed the Egyptian's house for Joseph's sake."*

Genesis 39:7-12 gives an account of the beginning of Joseph's adversity in Egypt. *"And it came to pass after these things, that his master's wife cast her eyes upon Joseph; and she said, Lie with me. But he refused, and said unto his master's wife, Behold, my master wotteth not what is with me in the house, and he hath committed all that he hath to my hand; There is none greater in this house than I; neither hath he kept back any thing from me but thee, because thou art his wife: how then can I do this great wickedness, and sin against God? And it came to pass, as she spake to Joseph day by day, that he hearkened not unto her, to lie by her, or to be with her. And it came to pass about this time, that Joseph went into the house to do his business; and there was none of the men of the house there within. And she caught him by his garment, saying, Lie with me: and he left his garment in her hand, and fled, and got him out."*
These verses tell us that Joseph resisted the sinful advances of Potiphar's wife. She even took hold of Joseph, so he ran, leaving his jacket in her hands. In retaliation, she took Joseph's coat to her husband and said that Joseph tried to assault her.

I contend that Joseph resisted when he should have avoided. The sad thing about this account is that Joseph resisted Potiphar's wife, but he did not try to avoid her. The Bible says, *"And there was none of the men of the house there within."* What in the world was Joseph doing in a house all alone with a woman whom he knew was after him **daily**? Joseph would never have had to resist if he had avoided being alone with Potiphar's wife.

I believe Potiphar's wife was probably very beautiful. Because Potiphar had position and money, he probably would have his choice of women. No doubt he would have chosen a wife for her beauty, and Joseph had placed himself in a situation where he knew a beautiful woman was trying to seduce him. A person with good character

CHARACTER AND THE SENSE TO AVOID

should always want to protect his reputation.

Genesis 39:10 says that *"day by day"* Potiphar's wife tempted Joseph. No doubt he realized that she was watching for an opportunity to have her way. Joseph knew that she was tempting him. The Bible says he refused to do such wickedness against his employer. Joseph placed himself in a situation where he had to resist sin when he could have avoided sin.

Had he been avoiding sin, he would have no doubt avoided the house completely. He surely would not have been in the house alone with Potiphar's wife, especially knowing that she was trying to entice him. Joseph should never have come face to face with that temptation. Yes, he did say "No!" to sin; however, he placed himself in a situation that could have destroyed him.

In the same way, the Devil wants you and is watching for his chance to get you. The Devil will make you an offer the same way Joseph was made an offer. He might not use the same circumstances, but be assured that the Devil will tempt you. You will not have to resist the committing of sin if you will avoid sin's territory. The Bible says in I Thessalonians 5:22, *"Abstain from all appearance of evil."*

1. It is easier to avoid temptation than it is to resist temptation. The disease of leprosy is often spoken of in the Bible. Leprosy is a fatal disease which is very contagious. Because lepers were cast out of cities, they often went hungry. A businessman with an open shop would always keep a long pole nearby so that if a leper approached his place of business, he could use that pole to keep the leper away. That shopkeeper did not use a short pole; he used a long pole to avoid contracting leprosy. Sin is far more dangerous and fatal than leprosy ever could be.

In my preaching, I often use an illustration about having a cobra with a four-foot striking range. I ask my audience, "How many of you would stand exactly four feet and one inch from that cobra?" My audience usually doesn't answer me back, but I would venture to say that most of them think, "That is ridiculous and stupid!" It is just as ridiculous to see how close you can get to sin because the bite of sin is more deadly than any poisonous snake. If someone gave you twelve ounces of strychnine and you knew that amount was fatal, you surely

CHARACTER

wouldn't try drinking five ounces to see what would happen. That would be ridiculous! Sin is far more fatal than any poison found on the face of this Earth today. **Do not resist sin. Avoid it!**

2. When you resist sin instead of avoiding it, others will still think you committed sin. Potiphar believed Joseph was guilty of assault. The accusations were not true, but Joseph knowingly put himself in a situation where he looked guilty. He lost not only his reputation, but his position, his job, his freedom, and his testimony — all because he resisted instead of avoided. The way **not** to have fleas is not sleeping with the dogs. The way **not** to smell like a pig is to refrain from playing with the pigs. If you are not guilty, do not look guilty. If you avoid sin, people usually won't believe you committed a sin.

If I told you I saw a Christian you admire in a state of drunkenness, you would say, "Far from it!" Why? Because someone who is far from sin is avoiding sin. If you are a Christian who is known for only resisting sin, someone will think that you are guilty. Your story will sound just like the one everybody else gives. Most guilty people always say, "I was there, but I am not guilty." When you are not guilty but you are in a place full of guilty people, your story sounds just like the one they give.

Live in such a way that you are not in the vicinity of sin. Reason with me. It is better to say, "I wasn't there," than to say, "I was there, but I'm not guilty." I would far rather say, "I'm not guilty of resisting. I am guilty of avoiding."

- If you do not want people to think you are guilty of criticism, don't run with the critics.
- If you don't want people to think that you are an immoral young lady, don't spend your time with a young man who has a bad reputation.
- If you don't want people to think that you are a rule breaker, don't spend your time with those who break the rules.
- If you don't want people to think that you are guilty of stealing, then stay away from other people's possessions. Avoid the appearance of sin!
- If you don't want people to think that you are guilty of being

CHARACTER AND THE SENSE TO AVOID

a rebel, then don't listen to the rebel's music.
- If you don't want people to think that you are a drunkard, then don't go to the office Christmas party where you know drinks will be served.

Avoid these situations or be pinned and labeled as guilty. Don't lose your reputation over something you did not do by putting your reputation on the line of resistance.

3. It is easier to avoid sin than it is to resist it. Don't let the Devil lie to you and make you think that you are strong enough to resist because you are not. Many of you sincerely plan to say "No!" when you come face to face with sin, but you are only strong enough to **avoid** sin. Most Christians are not strong enough to **resist**. Remember, you are only strong enough to avoid.

Many of you wonder why you leave church with a burning desire to say "No!" to sin but soon find yourself in sin. Quite simply, it is because you are not avoiding sin; you are hoping to resist it. Pride causes a Christian to think he is strong enough to resist sin. Avoiding sin is what makes you strong, and avoiding is what will revitalize your strength.

I have a confession: I do not have one credit card in my wallet. If I owned a credit card, I could not resist spending money, so I avoid the temptation of owning one. I have another confession: I have some former friends with whom I realize I am not strong enough to associate, so I avoid them altogether. Another confession: I don't have a "hella"vision in my home because I am not a good enough Christian to resist watching programs I should not watch. I am not a good enough Christian to turn the television off when I should be working. I happen to know me, so I avoid instead of resisting.

    I contend . . .
       . . . it is easier to say "No!" to going to an office Christmas party than to say "No!" to a beer at the Christmas party.
       . . . it is easier to say "No!" to the family's New Year's party than to say "No!" to the dirty videos they will show.
       . . . it is easier to say "No!" to the bad crowd than to say

"No!" to the criticism when a part of the bad crowd criticizes.

. . . it is easier to say "No!" to a ride in an old friend's car than to say "No!" to the rock music that will be played in the car.

. . . it is easier to say "No!" to a pack of cigarettes on the store counter than it is to say "No!" when the cigarettes are in your purse or pocket.

. . . it is easier to say "No!" to a date with an ungodly member of the opposite sex than to say "No!" when wicked requests are made.

. . . it is easier to say "No!" to a filthy magazine at the bookstore than when you have it hidden at home.

I have been accused of making the Christian life seem so easy. Why? Because quite simply, I **avoid** sin. I do not fight the battles that many Christians must fight. If I did, there is no way I could win because I **know** me. I know that I am a dirty, rotten, lowdown, good-for-nothing, filthy sinner. I know that if I am going to succeed in the Christian life, I must **avoid** sin's territory.

4. If you do not avoid sin and only resist it, the next step is to commit sin. I believe that if Joseph had been pardoned and allowed to return to work for Potiphar, he probably would have placed himself in the same situation again. I also believe he would eventually have committed a sexual sin. A Christian cannot play tag with sin and win. The next step after resisting is committing. If a Christian will avoid sin, he will not have to resist the sin, and that will keep the Christian from committing sin.

The problem simply stated is this: Everybody enjoys temptation. Most Christians wouldn't buy the *National Smut Paper*, but how many enjoy spending time in the checkout line at the store reviewing the headlines? Because we have a sin nature, we want to get close enough to enjoy and resist the temptation. We don't want to commit a sin, but we still get a thrill in saying we resisted. There is no physical thrill involved in avoiding sin. The farther from sin a Christian stays, the better off he will be.

5. Pray, *"Lead us not into temptation."* Matthew 6:13a says,

CHARACTER AND THE SENSE TO AVOID

"And lead us not into temptation." This verse is asking God to help us to avoid temptation. If I avoid, I have automatically resisted the temptation. I believe Joseph could have done better for himself by not being unchaperoned in Potiphar's house. Yes, Joseph did resist; nonetheless, I believe he could have and should have avoided the appearance of evil.

Chapter 20

Character and One of the Surest Ways Not to Get It

IN JAMES 3:1-6 THE BIBLE says, *"My brethren, be not many masters, knowing that we shall receive the greater condemnation. For in many things we offend all. If any man offend not in word, the same is a perfect man, and able also to bridle the whole body. Behold, we put bits in the horses' mouths, that they may obey us; and we turn about their whole body. Behold also the ships, which though they be so great, and are driven of fierce winds, yet are they turned about with a very small helm, whithersoever the governor listeth. Even so the tongue is a little member, and boasteth great things. Behold, how great a matter a little fire kindleth! And the tongue is a fire, a world of iniquity: so is the tongue among our members, that it defileth the whole body, and setteth on fire the course of nature; and it is set on fire of hell."*

When my sister and I were younger, my father bought us a pony. My sister was scared to death of that pony, and she wouldn't ride it. When she got a little bit older, my dad decided that my sister was going to learn to ride that pony. He instructed her, "Get up on that pony, grab the reins, and everything will be all right." After she had mounted the pony, one of my brothers stomped the ground, yelled, "Heeyah!" and that pony took off! I vividly remember that pony running wild across the field! My sister was screaming at the top of her lungs, "Dad! Help me! I'm gonna die!" She forgot all my dad's instructions. She forgot all about holding those reins. She was holding

CHARACTER

on for her life! Finally, we got hold of the dragging reins and brought the pony to a halt. Now bringing my sister under control was a different matter!

We were able to bring that pony under control because those reins were attached to a small, curbed piece of metal called a bit. When we put pressure on that bit, the pony began acquiescing to our desires. James 3:3 says that if you put a bit in the horse's mouth, you can control the horse, even though it is much larger than you. James 3:4 speaks of a ship being controlled by a helm — just a little device in comparison to the rest of the ship. James 3:5 says the tongue is a little member; but if you want to learn to bridle your whole body, you must learn to control your tongue. **One of the surest ways to get the character to control your body is to control your tongue.** One of the surest ways not to get character is to let your tongue run free. The Bible teaches that if we learn to control our tongue, controlling the rest of the body comes easier. Control your tongue, and most other things will be easy to conquer. One way people lose control of their tongues is by becoming critical or scornful. In counseling people throughout the years, I have met people I would label as being critical.

Why People Scorn

Basically, there are three reasons why characterless people scorn or criticize.

1. They enjoy being critical. The first part of Proverbs 1:22 says, *"How long, ye simple ones, will ye love simplicity? and the scorners delight in their scorning...?"* Scorners delight in their contempt and disdain. The Bible says gossips like to spread rumors. The gossip is someone who spends his time using his mouth to tear down rather than build. Critics will deny enjoying having a critical spirit. Some of their statements are, "I hate to tell you this _____"; or "I guess somebody has to tell you _____; I just wish it weren't me"; or "It kills me to have to tell you this _____"; or "I don't like to be the one, but **somebody** must tell you _____." Critics might even resort to prayer with a statement like, "We must pray for John Doe. He and his wife are having problems — you know what kind." Critics are

CHARACTER AND ONE OF THE SUREST WAYS NOT TO GET IT

liars whose criticizing always hides behind the lie of "somebody has got to do it."

2. They are proud. Proverbs 21:24a says, *"Proud and haughty scorner is his name."* People criticize because they think they are better than others. I've noticed that when a critic attacks someone, he usually compliments his victim **before** he criticizes him. He pats him on the head before he stabs him in the back. The critic might make a statement like, "Well, he's a much better Christian than I am **but** _____ " (then comes the criticism); or "I know he's busy in the Lord's work, but _____ " (then comes the criticism). Do these statements sound familiar? A critic feels superior, so he does his best to make sure that everyone else knows that he **is** superior.

3. They cannot control their temper. Proverbs 21:24b says, *"Who dealeth in proud wrath."* Because critics are full of pride, they can't control their tempers. "I'm mad and proud of it" is their attitude. Your temper is out of control because you are a gossip and a scorner. You are full of pride, and you enjoy every minute of it. Show me someone with an uncontrolled temper, and I will show you a critic.

The Critic's Expectations

There are four consequences of being a characterless critic.

1. The critic can expect a lack of God's blessing. Psalm 1:1 says, *"Blessed is the man that walketh not in the counsel of the ungodly, nor standeth in the way of sinners, nor sitteth in the seat of the scornful."* In this verse the Bible says that God has blessings for His people who do not sit in the seat of the scornful. A critic will experience an absence of God's blessings. A scorner will lose the benefit of seeing things built or people built because he is too busy using his mouth to tear down people. If you check the critic's spiritual life, you will find very little fruit.

2. The critic can expect God's judgment on his life. The Bible tells us in Proverbs 19:29 that *"Judgments are prepared for scorners, and stripes for the back of fools."* I believe God has specifically designed judgments which He has prepared for critics and gossips. Once when I was teaching this material at a church, I was verbally

CHARACTER

attacked by a man at that church for teaching these principles on scorners. As a matter of fact, he let everyone know what he thought about me. This church member called me at four o'clock in the morning and said, "Brother Owens, I must talk to you. You said there were specific judgments prepared for a critic. I didn't believe what you were teaching. You made me so angry that I bad-mouthed you all night long. About an hour ago, my mouth started burning, and blisters started forming inside my mouth. I thought I was going to choke to death. Then I remembered what you said about God having special judgments for someone who is a gossip. I got on my knees and asked God to forgive me. I started feeling better, and I wanted to call to apologize and ask your forgiveness."

Some of you say, "Brother Owens, do you really expect me to believe that?" or "Brother Owens, I have said bad things about people and nothing has ever happened to me." Have you ever heard this principle before? It just may be that God has been merciful to you until now. Don't risk God's judgment on your life by being a critic.

3. The critic can expect the destruction of his ability to comprehend wisdom. Proverbs 14:6a says, *"A scorner seeketh wisdom, and findeth it not."* The Bible is teaching in this verse that a critic is destroying his mind when he criticizes. A critic seeks wisdom and cannot find it. A gossip is unable to comprehend the wisdom of God. A critic puts another's problems into his mind that he cannot solve. So what does he have? He has an unfinished task in his mind. If the critic keeps filling his mind with unfinished tasks, he will destroy his mind. Why start something in your mind that you cannot finish?

"Brother Owens, I just can't seem to get anything out of my Bible reading." Ask yourself, "Am I a critic?" You may say, "I don't get anything out of the church services." Are you a critic? Perhaps you feel that this teaching doesn't apply to you. If you are a critic, you cannot comprehend the words of this chapter.

4. A critic will be lonely. Proverbs 9:12 says, *"If thou be wise, thou shalt be wise for thyself: but if thou scornest, thou alone shalt bear it."* Do you remember those special judgments of which I wrote in point #2? It would be bad enough to have the judgment of God for being a critic, but adding to that having to bear His judgment alone would be worse. Did you realize that you are going to isolate yourself? No one wants to be around a critic because a critic spares no one. If he will talk bad to you about someone, he will more than likely talk bad to someone about you. Proverbs 24:9b teaches us that criticism will cause people to hate you. *"The scorner is an abomination to men."* Did you know that everybody hates critics — even critics? Critics are very lonely people because nobody trusts them.

A critic will use his criticism to try to gain friends. Have you heard statements like, "I'll share this with you, but I couldn't with anyone else"; or, "Let's keep this between the two of us"? Real friendship can't have sin as a common denominator.

The Critic's Cure

The Bible gives several ways to fight being a critic. If a person has trouble with his tongue in the area of criticism, he ought to employ these five steps daily.

1. Avoid other critics. In Romans 16:17 the Bible says, *"Now I beseech you, brethren, mark them which cause divisions and offenses contrary to the doctrine which ye have learned; and avoid them."* Stay away from people whom you know will pull you down and cause you to say things you ought not to say.

2. Talk right. Psalm 19:14 says, *"Let the words of my mouth, and the meditation of my heart, be acceptable in thy sight, O LORD, my strength, and my redeemer."* Have you heard the old saying, "If you can't say anything good, don't say anything at all"? Go by it!

3. Confess your sin of criticism to God. I John 1:9 teaches, *"If we confess our sins, he is faithful and just to forgive us our sins, and to cleanse us from all unrighteousness."* Ask God to forgive you for each instance of criticism. Ask forgiveness for giving a critical report.

4. Memorize Scriptures about criticism. Psalm 119:11 says, *"Thy word have I hid in mine heart, that I might not sin against thee."* Do a Bible study on controlling your mouth to help in your thought life. *"For out of the abundance of the heart the mouth*

CHARACTER

speaketh." (Matthew 12:34b)

5. Ask God to help you. *"I can do all things through Christ which strengtheneth me."* (Philippians 4:13)

One of the surest ways not to have character is to refuse to control your tongue. God will never be able to use you like He wants to use you until you cease to be a critic or a gossip. No person wants to spend his life being lonely, unable to comprehend wisdom, having God's judgment on his life, and having a lack of God's blessings.

Chapter 21

Character and Our Strength

IN II SAMUEL 22:36b, DAVID SAID, *"And thy gentleness hath made me great."* Consider the source of this statement. David was a mighty and valiant warrior who killed a lion and a bear with his bare hands — David who fought and killed the giant Goliath. Songs were written about his accomplishments. *"Saul hath slain his thousands, and David his ten thousands."* (I Samuel 21:11b)

David did not believe he was great because he had battled and slain ten thousand. He did not believe he was great because he had conquered many. Nor did he think he was great because he ruled a kingdom. He didn't believe he was great because people feared him. A ruler as powerful as David would be feared by many.

1. David demonstrated his character by exhibiting gentleness. Real gentleness is *power under restraint.* Many have the mistaken concept that if a person is gentle, he has no power. That is not true. When lightning is flashing throughout the sky, it is unrestrained and unusable. Granted, that uncontrolled lightning is powerful. Regardless of how powerful that lightning is, if that electricity is not harnessed and brought under control, it is **destructive** instead of being **productive.** When power flows through an extension cord, it is under control. Electricity that is restricted is productive.

A person who possesses true gentleness is someone who has power and keeps his power under control. Let me illustrate: A person can open a door with a key or a crowbar. The person who opens the door

CHARACTER

properly with a key exercises control.

If a person cannot control his strength, he is no better than a weakling who has no strength. Both are unproductive. The weakling has no strength to restrain. The person who has not harnessed his strength has only destructive power. David realized that having gentleness — power under restraint — made him great.

2. David demonstrated the character when he gave up personal victory to help another. I Samuel 24:1-3 gives an account of David fleeing from Saul. *"And it came to pass, when Saul was returned from following the Philistines, that it was told him, saying, Behold, David is in the wilderness of En-gedi. Then Saul took three thousand chosen men out of all Israel, and went to seek David and his men upon the rocks of the wild goats. And he came to the sheepcotes by the way, where was a cave; and Saul went in to cover his feet: and David and his men remained in the sides of the cave."*

The Bible tells us that King Saul became David's enemy. David and his men were constantly fleeing from Saul and his armies. At one point David and his men took refuge from Saul in a cave. King Saul went to that very cave to rest. In all probability, if Saul had known David was in the cave, he would have killed David. When David saw the sleeping Saul, he knew he could have killed Saul on the spot.

In fact, David's men wanted him to kill Saul, but David said, *"...The LORD forbid that I should do this thing unto my master, the LORD'S anointed, to stretch forth mine hand against him, seeing he is the anointed of the LORD."* (I Samuel 24:6) David was not afraid of Saul; David knew he could not harm God's man. He exercised great restraint in sparing Saul, the would-be murderer.

When David confronted Saul at the cave and Saul realized the depth of David's graciousness, Saul wept and said, *" ... Thou art more righteous than I: for thou hast rewarded me good, whereas I have rewarded thee evil. And thou hast shewed this day how that thou hast dealt well with me: forasmuch as when the LORD had delivered me into thine hand, thou killedst me not."* (I Samuel 24:17, 18) David gave up having victory over Saul in order to have a good testimony and to help others. If permission had been granted to kill King Saul, Saul's followers would have been hurt.

Too often we want to prove another wrong — not as a help to that person, but so he will see we are right. With many, the issue is not **what** is right or wrong, but **who** is right or wrong. This attitude of superiority hurts people desperately.

My three sons, Jeffery II, Joshua, and Jeremiah, and I sometimes play basketball together. They are all three under the age of 12. We always play on the same team. We might even play as a team against some high school- or college-age players. I guarantee you that we get beat every time, but I am willing to lose while playing ball with my boys to teach them how to play ball. I believe that someday when the Owens boys are older, they will have victory on the court because they have learned proper procedures and ball handling.

3. David demonstrated the character to listen when told to control his strength. I Samuel 25:32 and 33 says, *"And David said to Abigail, Blessed be the LORD God of Israel, which sent thee this day to meet me: And blessed be thy advice, and blessed be thou, which has kept me this day from coming to shed blood, and from avenging myself with mine own hand."* David had sent envoys to Nabal asking for sustenance for his men. David had protected Nabal's men and his flocks in the wilderness. In fact, he had not even allowed his hungry men to take any of Nabal's animals for food. The Bible says Nabal was *"churlish and evil in his doings,"* and he contemptuously refused David's request.

David prepared his men to do battle with Nabal. However, word reached Abigail, Nabal's wife, of the impending battle because of Nabal's lack of consideration. Abigail had food prepared and loaded on the backs of donkeys and rode to meet David and his men. When Abigail met David, she bowed before him, fell at his feet, and said, *"Upon me, my lord, upon me let this iniquity be: and let thine handmaid, I pray thee, speak in thine audience, and hear the words of thine handmaid."* (v. 24) Abigail told David she did not see his representatives and confessed that she knew Nabal was a wicked man, *"a man of Belial."* Still she asked David not to shed more blood and avenge himself. David heard and accepted her plea and said, *"Blessed be the LORD God of Israel, which sent thee this day to meet me: And blessed be thy advice, and blessed be thou, which has kept me this day from coming to shed blood ....*" David received her peace offering and spared her husband and home.

A great person will listen to others who say, "Calm down." If you are truly great, you will listen to someone who is trying to help you control your power. Psalm 141:5 teaches that a righteous person can be a calming influence. *"Let the righteous smite me; it shall be a kindness: and let him reprove me; it shall be an excellent oil, which shall not break my head: for yet my prayer also shall be in their calamities."*

James 3:17, *"But the wisdom that is from above is first pure, then peaceable, gentle, and easy to be intreated, full of mercy and good fruits, without partiality, and without hypocrisy."* Please notice the word *"gentle"* is followed by the words *"easy to be intreated."* People of character who have power will listen when a spouse or a friend or a pastor or a boss or a brother or a sister or the Holy Spirit reminds them to control their power.

4. David demonstrated character by not using revenge to obtain or keep his power. I Samuel 30:11-14 says, *"And they found an Egyptian in the field, and brought him to David, and gave him bread, and he did eat; and they made him drink water; And they gave him a piece of a cake of figs, and two clusters of raisins: and when he had eaten, his spirit came again to him: for he had eaten no bread, nor drunk any water, three days and three nights. And David said unto him, To whom belongest thou? and whence art thou? And he said, I am a young man of Egypt, servant to an Amalekite; and my master left me, because three days agone I fell sick. We made an invasion upon the south of the Cherethites, and upon the coast which belongeth to Judah, and upon the south of Caleb; and we burned Ziklag with fire."*

When David and his men were away from Ziklag, the Amalekite army destroyed the city and captured the people — mostly women and children. Two of the captives were David's own wives. When David and his men pursued the Amalekites, they found a wounded Egyptian in a field. Upon questioning the man, David found the Egyptian was a bondservant to an Amalekite and was left by his master to die. If David was like most men, he would have executed the Egyptian on

CHARACTER AND OUR STRENGTH

the spot; but, because he controlled himself and cared for the injured slave, David received needed information to attack the real enemy. David wanted more to do right than to have power.

5. David demonstrated character by wanting security with God more than he did with man. II Samuel 9:1-7 says, *"And David said, Is there yet any that is left of the house of Saul, that I may shew him kindness for Jonathan's sake? And there was of the house of Saul a servant whose name was Ziba. And when they had called him unto David, the king said unto him, Art thou Ziba? And he said, Thy servant is he. And the king said, Is there not yet any of the house of Saul, that I may shew the kindness of God unto him? And Ziba said unto the king, Jonathan hath yet a son, which is lame on his feet. And the king said unto him, Where is he? And Ziba said unto the king, Behold, he is in the house of Machir, the son of Ammiel, in Lo-debar. Then king David sent, and fetched him out of the house of Machir, the son of Ammiel, from Lo-debar. Now when Mephibosheth, the son of Jonathan, the son of Saul, was come unto David, he fell on his face, and did reverence. And David said, Mephibosheth. And he answered, Behold thy servant! And David said unto him, Fear not: for I will surely shew thee kindness for Jonathan thy father's sake, and will restore thee all the land of Saul thy father; and thou shalt eat bread at my table continually."*

This passage of Scripture shows David's continued reverence for the Lord's anointed. David wanted to know if there were any members of the house of Saul yet alive. Historically, any relatives of the former king usually would be put to death as a security precaution to prevent a future rebellion. David is told that Jonathan's son, a crippled boy named Mephibosheth, was still living. David sent to Lo-debar and brought not only Mephibosheth to live in royalty, but all his servants and their families. David also restored to Mephibosheth all the land and property in the house of Saul. Putting Mephibosheth and his family to death would have been acceptable. The destruction of the entire lineage of Saul would have augmented David's security and hold on the throne, but David didn't want or need the security offered by men; he knew his security was from God.

6. David demonstrated character by not hurting those who

CHARACTER

tried to hurt him with words. II Samuel 16:5-7 gives an account of a member of the house of Saul determined to hurt David. *"And when king David came to Bahurim, behold, thence came out a man of the family of the house of Saul, whose name was Shimei, the son of Gera: he came forth, and cursed still as he came. And he cast stones at David, and at all the servants of king David: and all the people and all the mighty men were on his right hand and on his left. And thus said Shimei when he cursed, Come out, come out, thou bloody man, and thou man of Belial."*

Because Shimei was cursing the king, David's friend Abishai wanted to kill Shimei. David wisely chose to ignore Shimei's abusive words. David was basically living by a saying commonly heard today: "Sticks and stones may break my bones, but names will never hurt me." I personally know of some marriages, churches, friends, and relatives who need character in this area of controlling their tongues like David.

7. God is a perfect example of power under control. A story is told of a man preaching in a park. As he was preaching, someone began mocking him from the back of the crowd, "Hey, preacher, there's no God. If there's a God, let Him kill me! Come on, God. You're not up there. You are a phony." That preacher replied, "Sir, when I was walking to this park today, a little boy about three foot tall came out of an alley — seemingly out of a garbage can, he was so unkempt. His clothing was torn and his face was dirty, and you could tell that he was a street kid. That little guy walked over to me, stuck his fist in my face, and said, 'Come on, mister. Fight me. Fight me.' If I had wanted to, I could have hit that boy with one blow and killed him. I could have sent that little boy into eternity. Instead, I knelt down, reached out, hugged him to me, and said, 'Little boy, why don't you let me buy you some new clothes and get you some new toys. Please let me feed you and help you.' "

That preacher looked at the heckler and said, "Sir, to God you are just like that little boy. If God chose to hit you, He could. If God chose to take your life right now, He could. Instead, God wants to love you and clothe you and help you."

Every one of us deserves to be dead. If every one of us got what

CHARACTER AND OUR STRENGTH

we deserved, we would all be dead and suffering in Hell. Think of all the times that you have turned your back on God and you have mocked Him. Perhaps you have scorned the preacher's words or you have talked against God's man. God could take your life at this very moment in any number of ways. However, God says, "I am going to control My power so that I can help those for whom I died."

God hates sin. If an almighty, holy God can control Himself with sinners, it would surely seem like we sinners could control ourselves when we are around other sinners.

Chapter 22

Character and Salvation

ECCLESIASTES 12:13 SAYS, *"Let us hear the conclusion of the whole matter: Fear God, and keep his commandments: for this is the whole duty of man."*

1. No man's character can save him. The Bible says in Ephesians 2:8 and 9, *"For by grace are ye saved through faith; and that not of yourselves: it is the gift of God: Not of works, lest any man should boast."* Titus 3:5a says, *"Not by works of righteousness which we have done, but according to his mercy he saved us."*

2. Every man is a sinner. Romans 3:10 says, *"As it is written, There is none righteous, no not one."* Romans 3:23 tells us, *"For all have sinned, and come short of the glory of God."*

3. There is a price man must pay for being a sinner. The Bible says in Hebrews 9:27, *"And as it is appointed unto men once to die, but after this the judgment."* Romans 5:12b tells us, *"And so death passed upon all men, for that all have sinned."* Romans 6:23a says, *"For the wages of sin is death."* Revelation 21:8b says, *"Shall have their part in the lake which burneth with fire and brimstone ...."*

4. God loved us and sent His son, Jesus Christ, to pay the price of sin for all men. The Bible tells us in John 3:16, *"For God so loved the world, that he gave his only begotten Son, that whosoever believeth in him should not perish, but have everlasting life."* Romans 5:8 says, *"But God commendeth his love toward us, in that, while we*

CHARACTER

were yet sinners, Christ died for us." Romans 6:23, *"For the wages of sin is death; but the gift of God is eternal life through Jesus Christ our Lord."*

5. To be saved, you must receive Jesus Christ as your Saviour and believe that His death was payment to God for your sin. Romans 10:9 says, *"That if thou shalt confess with thy mouth the Lord Jesus, and shalt believe in thine heart that God hath raised him from the dead, thou shalt be saved."* Acts 16:31a says, *"And they said, Believe on the Lord Jesus Christ, and thou shalt be saved."*

6. Jesus Christ paid your sin debt for you. A man of character should feel that it is his duty to get saved. Ecclesiastes 12:13b tells us, *"Fear God ... for this is the whole duty of man."* What terrible ingratitude to think God's Son would die for you so you could go to Heaven someday, and you choose to be of such low character that you won't accept Him as your Saviour, and you spend an eternity in Hell because of it!

7. Receive Christ as your Saviour; it is your duty. Won't you bow your head right now, wherever you are, and receive Jesus Christ as Saviour? Say this simple prayer or one of your own like it with a sincere heart:

> *"Dear Jesus, I know that I am a sinner and that I deserve to go to Hell. Please forgive me and come into my heart. I do now trust You to save me and then to take me to Heaven when I die. I'm trusting You and only You as my Saviour. Thank you for saving me."*

8. You are now surely saved if you trusted Christ as your Saviour. Our God is a God of great character. God cannot lie. He said He would save you; therefore, He is honor-bound to have kept His Word. Hebrews 6:18a says, *"... It was impossible for God to lie."*

9. Now that you are saved, you will remain that way. John 10:28 says, *"And I give unto them eternal life; and they shall never perish, neither shall any man pluck them out of my hand."* God is a God of character. He keeps His word, and He finishes what He starts. He does everything right the first time.

10. It is a saved person's duty to serve God. Ecclesiastes 12:13b says, *"...And keep his commandments...."*

It may be as important to teach a child character as it is to teach him the plan of salvation. If the child has been taught character, he will more than likely get saved because it is the right thing to do.

Chapter 23

Character and the Goal of Godly Leadership

PROVERBS 29:17-21 SAYS, *"Correct thy son, and he shall give thee rest; yea, he shall give delight unto thy soul. Where there is no vision, the people perish: but he that keepeth the law, happy is he. A servant will not be corrected by words: for though he understand he will not answer. Seest thou a man that is hasty in his words? there is more hope of a fool than of him. He that delicately bringeth up his servant from a child shall have him become his son at the length."*

Many people rise quickly to places of leadership. Many people also quickly fall. Many people would like to have a position of leadership, but very few would actually like to pay the necessary price to be a godly leader. Often someone who rises quickly to a place of leadership gets there by a means that will not sustain him when he gets to the top. Let me give you an example of such a person.

Adolf Hitler was a powerful man. He knew how to get things from people, and he knew how to challenge people. He knew how to rally people, and he knew how to excite people. However, all he really knew was how to dictate people. The type of leadership that advanced Hitler to the top would not sustain him after he arrived there.

I don't believe that we, as leaders, are to have the attitude of "whatever it takes to get the job done." That was a philosophy Hitler advocated. I do believe leaders are to have the attitude of "whatever it takes to get the job done within the realm of right." Therefore, if any goals you have set cannot be reached in God's way, those goals evidently are not God's goals.

Remember this statement: **Leadership is the ability to instill in the hearts of your followers a desire to follow.** The Bible describes three totally different people in Proverbs 29:17-21 — a father, a son, and a servant. This chapter deals primarily with those three different people and their intrinsic relationships.

First, let me digress to give an actual account which took place on January 7, 1961. A middle-aged couple named Harold and Shirley had two sons — Bob, age sixteen, and Larry, age fifteen. Bob was seemingly the favored son because he was talented in the area of athletics.

On January 6, 1961, Bob was playing in an away basketball game, so his brother Larry traveled along to watch the ballgame. At the conclusion of the game, Bob came home on the team bus, which arrived home at nine o'clock that evening. Larry was on the fan bus, which arrived an hour later. Larry's parents were very disturbed with him for getting home late. Therefore, he was punished severely; in fact, the way in which he was punished was ridiculously severe. Throughout the night, Larry planned to wreak revenge on his mother and father for their unfair correction.

That next morning Larry awakened early and went to the kitchen. When his mother Shirley entered the kitchen, Larry shot his mother five times — three times in the chest, two times in the back with a .22 rifle. When his father came rushing into the room, Larry shot him nine times — once in the jaw, once in the chest, three times in the arm, three times in the back, and once in the buttocks. In pure malice, Larry shot his dad the last few times as his father was sprawled on the floor. It is rare to find a child who will murder his parents; patricide and matricide are rare. Even in our wicked society, it does happen but, thankfully, not often. We will come back to this story at the end of this chapter. I want you to recognize some similarities between this actual newspaper account and the Bible teaching found in Proverbs 29 in which we see three people — a leader, a son, and a servant.

A leader must strive to go beyond having a servant-master relationship with people. For a leader to be a godly leader, he needs to understand there is more to leading than just saying, "I'm the master, and you're the servant." Some leaders wrongly think the followers are to bow down to them and do what they are told. There is a greater relationship than that available. That relationship is the relationship between a father and his son. The leaders of our world very desperately need character in this area.

I.
The Bible Explains the Relationship Between a Father, a Son, and a Servant

First there is a definite difference between a son and a servant. In Proverbs 29:17 note the words, *"Correct thy son."* In verse 19 notice, *"A servant will not be corrected by words."* In verse 20, the Bible says that there is more hope for a fool than for a leader who is hasty with his words.

A. The servant. The Bible says that a servant *"will not be corrected by words,"* which means a servant will not be corrected by words **only**. The servant may respond to a leader's harsh words of discipline. The follower may understand the words, and he may understand why he is being corrected; but if a leader is not careful and he is hasty with his words, the follower will respond on the outside. However, inwardly he will probably be very irritated with his leader's treatment. The follower will not really respond with his whole heart. He will do what he is told because he is forced to do what he is told.

Would it not be much better if a follower could do what he was told because he liked to do what he was told? A servant-master relationship often shows obedience on the outside while concealing hatred and a fear on the inside. That is the way Hitler led his people.

Have you ever had someone assume that you were going to obey, be loyal, and jump at any command? Maybe that leader even became hasty with his words. Inwardly, you probably wondered, "What right does he have to treat me this way?" Now I do not think for one minute a follower should inwardly seethe when he is told to do something, but I am trying to illustrate a real feeling people experience when a leader does not lead in God's way.

CHARACTER

I believe a follower ought to follow rightly. However, I also believe all leaders ought to lead rightly as well. That is exactly what this Scripture is teaching. Assuming that he has achieved a good enough relationship to correct someone bluntly if needed, a leader who is hasty to get what he wants has poor leadership. The follower may respond, but he is more than likely only going to follow with his hands and not with his heart.

B. The son. *"Correct thy son, and he shall give thee rest; yea, he shall give delight unto thy soul."* I have three sons and one daughter at home. I can spank any of them and the minute I'm finished spanking, they crawl into my lap. My children give delight to my soul. I can scold my children, and they will run to me and love me anyway. God says this is exactly how we ought to lead people. If ever followers are scolded, they will still love us after the scolding. They will obey with their hands and with their hearts; they obey inwardly, as well as outwardly.

Perhaps you thought you were a good leader because you had everybody terrified of you. You are not a good leader; you are a fool. I scold my kids, but they know that I love them. When my parents corrected me as a youth or expected some immediate obedience, I did not sit back and say, "Well, who do you think you are?" I loved my parents for instructing me. If you did not have the privilege of growing up in that type of environment, I sincerely wish you had because I know what it is like to grow up in the right atmosphere. My parents instructed me and corrected me, and I loved them anyway.

The goal of leadership is to take a servant relationship and turn it into a son relationship. One of the statements I love to hear Dr. Jack Hyles make the most is, "These men on my staff are just like my **sons**." Brother Hyles is a master at turning his servants into sons.

Recently I went on a preaching trip with him for three days to York, Pennsylvania. We walked through a mall together, and we were talking about the things of the Lord. He stopped right in the middle of that mall, put his arms around me, began to weep, and said, "Son, I'm very pleased with the things you are saying right now." I have been in the ministries of First Baptist Church of Hammond for 11 years. Brother Hyles has loved and cared for me; in the same token,

I love him — he is like a dad to me. I do not fear him in the slightest because he would never do anything to hurt me. I love and admire that kind of godly leadership. This story reminds me that people who were close to Brother Lester Roloff called him "Dad."

C. A servant or son to Christ. A servant relationship with Christ is different than a son relationship. Serving Christ because you feel you have to is not as productive as serving Christ because you get to serve Him or want to serve Him. He's my Heavenly Dad! I want the men who lead with me in my ministries to know I love them; I don't want them to be afraid of me. No person needs to fear me because no matter what, I love him. I plan on doing as much as I can for those who work with me.

II.
How to Turn a Servant into a Son

Let me share three ways I have found that will bring a servant toward sonship.

A. Be tender with people. Proverbs 29:21 teaches, *"He that delicately bringeth up his servant from a child shall have him become his son at the length."* The word *delicately* means *to use tenderness.* The Bible says, *"A soft answer turneth away wrath."* (Proverbs 15:1a) In Ephesians 6:4a the Bible says, *"And, ye fathers, provoke not your children to wrath."* A leader does not need to make his followers angry just to prove he is a man. A leader should love his followers and never want to raise his voice at a co-worker. A leader can choose to lead softly.

If a leader "chews out" a servant before he is a son, he has probably nipped the relationship in the bud, and the follower may never trust the leader again. He may serve and do what he is told, but he may despise the leader as a result. He will probably be the first one to stab the leader in the back. He will not like the leader because he is not likeable. That type of leader is not leading like Jesus. In the Bible, you will not find Jesus tearing off the disciples' heads every time He gave an order. Correction should be administered according to the relationship's stability.

These are principles to help you lead as a pastor or in any position. A leader is not supposed to be tooting his own horn; he is supposed to be leading. Any time a man has to walk around screaming, "I'm the leader here! I'm in charge of this thing!" he is merely saying, "I'm not the leader here, and I'm not in charge." Leadership is not just a title. A leader is something **you are**. If you have to throw around a title to prove what you are, you are not what you thought.

Turn your servants into sons. Why? You will rest better that way. I correct in love so I do not destroy the relationship's bond. I once heard someone say, "I make them or break them." I say, "Make them or make them."

Isaiah 61:1 says, *"The Spirit of the Lord GOD is upon me, because the LORD hath anointed me to preach good tidings unto the meek; he hath sent me to bind up the brokenhearted, to proclaim liberty to the captives, and the opening of the prison to them that are bound."* Note that Jesus is binding up that which was broken, not destroying God's people.

You cannot scare people into being loyal — that is not real loyalty. In order to be loyal, your people must love you. How do you achieve that? *"We love him, because he first loved us."* (I John 4:19) You must first love them! It is scriptural! This is Bible leadership in its purest form.

B. Train your people. Proverbs 29:21 says *"bringeth up,"* which means *training*. Leaders are responsible to teach the follower how to do right. Rather than exposing to them and everybody around you that you are the wonderful leader and they are stupid followers, maybe you ought to teach them how to follow successfully.

Have you ever been scolded for doing something wrong, and you didn't even know what you were doing? Perhaps no one had trained you or taught you, but you were getting in trouble anyway. As a leader, I have a policy I follow. Any time I see disobedience in the ranks with my co-workers, the first question I ask myself is, "Have I failed to train them correctly?" I would hate to discipline somebody for failing at something which was actually a direct result of my lack of character in training that person. I'm not going to verbally mistreat anyone because I am too petty to take the time to teach the person how to be successful. I want to teach my co-workers how to be successful. It is not my job to see what I can get out of them; it is my job to see what I can build in them. If I don't have the character to train, instruct, and love my co-workers, then I certainly do not have the right to lead.

C. Take time for your people. Proverbs 29:21 says *"at the length,"* which means *being patient* or *taking time.* So often we are willing to be patient — if we can do it quickly!

A common occurrence with many leaders is that they are in such a hurry to get all their personal fame and glory that they are not willing to pay the price to teach their people how to be successful. That kind of leader wants to make sure he looks good to the world — no matter what it takes to get there. That kind of leader also makes sure he gets what he wants. A leader is not going to be able to build lives in that way.

If you won't pay the price to train people for God, you must be training them for yourself. Possibly you think you are **god**. People will not become overnight successes like you think you did. You will not quickly convince someone to become your son; you cannot force that relationship. You will love followers into sonship with time, training, and tenderness.

I do not know about you, but I am somewhat delicate. My self-worth cannot handle having people verbally beat me around all the time. I need somebody to kindly encourage me, to love me, to teach me, and to train me. This training requires time because, in many cases, the people with whom you are working have already been spiritually abused by some irresponsible dictator masquerading as a leader. These followers are victims of people who do not practice good leadership; therefore, they use the methods of dictators to get what they want.

Some people will be slow in progressing to sonship. They will be slow to respond to your words. Just be patient with them. When someone has been bruised, he needs time to heal. Give him that time to heal. A leader must realize that many have been previously hurt.

Since God wants to use everyone to his fullest potential, a leader has no right to discard a follower along the way.

III.
Results of Turning a Servant into a Son

A. Good rest. The Bible says that turning a servant into a son will *"give you rest."* You may rest with the confidence that these sons will allow you to be the leader. I don't spend any of my time wondering if somebody in my ranks is trying to take over, betray, or hurt me. I do not experience these worries; I rest well. Since I am not out to hurt anybody, I rest well, knowing the ministry I am building is strong! If you do things God's way, it will turn out much better than doing it man's way. A leader with these character traits rests well.

I rest, knowing followers are being trained. I rest, knowing God is pleased. I rest well, knowing that I have had the privilege of building a quality in a person that will stay with him the rest of his life and will help make him a success, **no matter what comes**.

B. Delight to your soul. Proverbs 29:17b says, *"He shall give delight unto thy soul."* The spirit communicates with God, and the soul is what communicates with man. When the Bible speaks of *"delight unto thy soul,"* it means that you can have delightful human relationships.

Someone has said that you cannot be right with God if you are not right with your parents. If you will follow the teaching of developing a father-son relationship as put forth in this chapter, you can heal your own relationship with your parents.

Conclusion

Because it is a very rare happening, most people who hear of a child who murders his parents are appalled and shocked. As a general rule, children do not want to kill their parents. In the same token, you would be shocked to know how often I find followers who have taken

CHARACTER AND THE GOAL OF GODLY LEADERSHIP

all they can with their leaders because they feel abused. Certainly, if you are a follower, you should follow. Be a good son-trainee. Please don't let a few poor "fathers" ruin your growth in life.

Remember the story earlier in this chapter about the murdered parents? According to the book of Proverbs, our goal is to take our servants and turn them into our sons. That story is a very tragic story to me because I see someone who has taken a son and turned him into a servant — these parents actually reversed the process!

I wonder how many people started out being good servants and were driven away and never developed the son relationship because of poor leadership. Please pay the price to be a godly leader. Not everybody is willing to develop his character is this area.

Chapter 24

Character and Being a Martyr for Your Marriage

IN EPHESIANS 5:21-25 THE BIBLE says, *"Submitting yourselves one to another in the fear of God. Wives, submit yourselves unto your own husbands, as unto the Lord. For the husband is the head of the wife, even as Christ is the head of the church: and he is the saviour of the body. Therefore as the church is subject unto Christ, so let the wives be to their own husbands in every thing. Husbands, love your wives, even as Christ also loved the church, and gave himself for it."*

God compares the relationship between the husband and wife to Christ and the church. The Bible says that Christ gave Himself for the church. One reason for so many catastrophes in marriage and so many divorces today is because people do not want to heed the admonition of Ephesians 5:25. Partners in marriage must be willing to die for each other just as Christ died for the church. Christ loved the church and gave Himself for it.

Let me ask you a question: Would you die for Christ? Someone has said, "Anybody could die for Christ. The hard part is living for Him." I beg to differ with the person who made that statement. I would rather live than die any day. I would say that most feel that way basically. Therefore, you had better marry someone who loves Christ and the church. If your mate does not love Christ, what real training does he have to love you? The husband is to be willing to die for Christ, and, in the same token, he should be willing to die for his wife.

Therefore, you had better marry someone who loves the church and loves Christ. If your spouse does not love Christ, what real training does he have to love you? Your husband needs to be willing to die for Christ, and he should be willing to die for you.

Martyrs for the Faith

I believe these historical examples of people who died for Christ should teach a couple to be willing to die for each other. Possessing strong Biblical character would produce a good marriage partner — one willing to die for Christ. Martyrs are people who predetermine that they will die for a cause. They didn't just **happen** to die for some cause. Decide that when you get married that you will stay married for life.

Revelation 20:4 says people were beheaded for the cause of Christ. *"I saw thrones, and they sat upon them, and judgment was given unto them: and I saw the souls of them that were beheaded for the witness of Jesus, and for the word of God ...."*

Acts 7:54-60 gives an account of the first martyr mentioned in the Bible. *"When they heard these things, they were cut to the heart, and they gnashed on him with their teeth. But he, being full of the Holy Ghost, looked up stedfastly into heaven, and saw the glory of God, and Jesus standing on the right hand of God, And said, Behold, I see the heavens opened, and the Son of man standing on the right hand of God. Then they cried out with a loud voice, and stopped their ears, and ran upon him with one accord, And cast him out of the city, and stoned him: and the witnesses laid down their clothes at a young man's feet, whose name was Saul. And they stoned Stephen, calling upon God, and saying, Lord Jesus, receive my spirit. And he kneeled down, and cried with a loud voice, Lord, lay not this sin to their charge. And when he had said this, he fell asleep."* **Stephen** was stoned to death for the cause of Christ. Could you have that kind of commitment to your spouse?

James, one of the Sons of Thunder, a son of Zebedee, was beheaded for Christ. **Philip**, the first to be called a disciple, was flogged 39 times with a cat-o'-nine-tails, imprisoned, and then crucified. **Matthew**, the toll collector or tax man, was slain with a halberd, a weapon which had an ax-like blade and a steel spike mounted on the end of a long shaft.

James, at the age of 94, was battered and stoned, and his brains were beaten out with a fuller's club, a blacksmith's tool used to crush iron. He says in James 1:3, *"Knowing this, that the trying of your faith worketh patience."* James goes on to say in verse 6, *"But let him ask in faith, nothing wavering. For he that wavereth is like a wave of the sea driven with the wind and tossed."* James did not waver in his faith.

Matthias was stoned at Jerusalem and then beheaded. I call that commitment! **Andrew**, the brother of Peter, was crucified on the cross. His cross was laid on the side as he was crucified. **Mark**, a convert of Peter, was dragged to pieces by people in the city of Alexandria.

Peter was crucified upside-down because he said he was not worthy to die in the same way his Saviour died. Sixteen times in the books of Peter, the word *"suffering"* is mentioned. I Peter 4:13 says, *"But rejoice, inasmuch as ye are partakers of Christ's sufferings: that, when his glory shall be revealed, ye may be glad also with exceeding joy."* These verses speak of having deep commitment — enough for which to die.

"Beloved, think it not strange concerning the fiery trial which is to try you, as though some strange thing happened unto you." (I Peter 4:12) What are those *"fiery trials"*? History chronicles how Emperor Nero would take Christians, bind them, and place them on a 12-foot platform in his flower garden, where they were doused in tar and then set afire — human wicks to light the flower garden. Why? So drunken whoremongers could examine the beautiful flowers while at Nero's parties! Do you have commitment — the same type of commitment to your mate as these Christians did for Christ?

Paul had his throat cut with a sword. In II Corinthians 1:5 he writes, *"For as the sufferings of Christ abound in us, so our consolation also aboundeth by Christ."* He also writes, *"We are troubled on every side, yet not distressed; we are perplexed, but not* *in despair; Persecuted, but not forsaken; cast down, but not destroyed; Always bearing about in the body the dying of the Lord Jesus, that the life also of Jesus might be made manifest in our body. For we which live are alway delivered unto death for Jesus' sake, that the life also of Jesus might be made manifest in our mortal flesh."* (II Corinthians 4:8-11) Paul had a **commitment** to Christ.

II Corinthians 6:4-11 says, *"But in all things approving ourselves as the ministers of God, in much patience, in afflictions, in necessities, in distresses, In stripes, in imprisonments, in tumults, in labours, in watchings, in fastings; By pureness, by knowledge, by longsuffering, by kindness, by the Holy Ghost, by love unfeigned, By the word of truth, by the power of God, by the armour of righteousness on the right hand and on the left, By honour and dishonour, by evil report and good report: as deceivers, and yet true: ... As sorrowful, yet alway rejoicing; as poor, yet making many rich; as having nothing, and yet possessing all things. O ye Corinthians, our mouth is open unto you, our heart is enlarged."* Upon coming to Macedonia, Paul said their flesh had no rest; they were troubled on every side. Paul was committed to the cause of Christ.

Paul addresses what he suffered for Christ's sake in II Corinthians 11:23-28 and 12:7 which says, *"Are they ministers of Christ? (I speak as a fool) I am more; in labours more abundant, in stripes above measure, in prisons more frequent, in deaths oft. Of the Jews five times received I forty stripes save one. Thrice was I beaten with rods, once was I stoned, thrice I suffered shipwreck, a night and a day I have been in the deep; In journeys often, in perils of waters, in perils of robbers, in perils by mine own countrymen, in perils by the heathen, in perils in the city, in perils in the wilderness, in perils in the sea, in perils among false brethren; In weariness and painfulness, in watchings often, in hunger and thirst, in fastings often, in cold and nakedness. Beside those things that are without, that which cometh upon me daily, the care of all the churches. And lest I should be exalted above measure through the abundance of the revelations, there was given to me a thorn in the flesh...."*

The Bible says a husband is to love his wife like Christ loved the church! The following are more examples of men who showed us how

CHARACTER AND BEING A MARTYR FOR YOUR MARRIAGE

much they loved Christ.

Jude was crucified; but he said in Jude 3, *"Beloved, when I gave all diligence to write unto you of the common salvation, it was needful for me to write unto you, and exhort you that ye should earnestly contend for the faith ...."* In other words, Jude was going to fight for the church. So ought you to learn to fight for your marriage. Some wife needs to fight for her husband, and some husband needs to fight for his wife instead of fighting with each other.

Bartholomew was cruelly beaten and crucified. **Thomas** was thrust through with a spear by pagan priests. **Luke** was hanged on an olive tree. **Simon** was crucified. **John**, the beloved disciple, survived boiling in a cauldron of oil, but he said, *"Remember the word that I said unto you, The servant is not greater than his lord. If they have persecuted me, they will also persecute you."* (John 15:20a)

Timothy rebuked some people for celebrating pagan feasts, and they beat him with clubs. History records that he died two days later, probably from internal hemorrhaging.

Ignatius, a follower of Peter as the bishop of Antioch, was thrown to wild beasts. He said, "I am the wheat of Christ. I am going to be ground with the teeth of wild beasts that I may be found faithful. I would rather die for Christ than rule the whole earth." Would you rather die for your wife than to rule the whole earth?

Jonah was told to go to Nineveh; however, he ran from God's will. I believe Jonah had a reason to run! The welcome most preachers received in Nineveh was torture. It is said that spears were driven into the ground and the prophets of God were impaled on those spears like a human popsicle. The tormentors would continue by taking razor-sharp pieces of stone or glass and cutting strips of flesh, which were grabbed with pliers. In this way, the flesh was stripped from a man. No wonder Jonah didn't want to go to Nineveh! Of course, we know that Jonah went and preached a great revival. Why? He had a commitment to the cause of Christ.

Polycarp had his life threatened by Marcus Aurelius. Finally two of Aurelius' soldiers caught him. Polycarp asked, "May I pray before my destruction?" When they said, "Yes," he fell on his face before God and prayed the power of God down, such that the soldiers were

CHARACTER

struggling to get away from him because the power of God was so evident on his life! They said, "We'll have no part of having this man crucified!" Polycarp was sentenced to be burned at the stake. His captors asked him if he wanted to be nailed to the stake, and he said, "The One Whom I am willing to die for will not have to worry about me running from the fire." Let me ask you a question: Does your spouse have the confidence to say my mate won't run from a fiery trial in our marriage?

Alexander was beaten with staves, torn with hooks, and burnt with fire. **Theodora**, a young, beautiful lady in Antioch was commanded to sacrifice to a false god. When she refused, she was beheaded, and her body was burned. Acts 11:26b says that they were called "Christians" first at Antioch. *"And the disciples were called Christians first in Antioch."*

When **Saturnius** refused to sacrifice to idols, he was tied by the feet to a bull's tail and dragged by the enraged animal down the temple steps until his head was completely empty of brains.

Maxima, **Dontillia**, and **Secunda** were three women who would not deny Christ. They were forced to drink gall and vinegar, scourged and tormented on the gallows, rubbed with lime, scorched on a gridiron, and pushed within inches of their deaths by wild beasts. Why? For the cause of the church and for the cause of Christ!

Quintin was stretched with pulleys until all of his joints were dislocated. He was beaten with wire scourges and boiled in oil. His wounds were covered with hot pitch and tar, and torches were placed in his armpits.

Romanus, a deacon at the church in Sisera, was scourged and put on a rack. His body was torn with hooks, he was cut with knives, and, a little at a time, all the skin was scraped from his face. His hair was pulled out by the roots. His teeth were beaten from their sockets one at a time, and he was finally strangled to death.

Saturninus, a pastor in Africa, was tortured in prison and starved to death, and all four of his children chose to follow in his steps.

Bishop Basil's body was ordered torn into seven different parts.

The list of those who were martyred for the cause of Christ is endless. Foxe's *Book of Martyrs* lists hundreds of people who were

CHARACTER AND BEING A MARTYR FOR YOUR MARRIAGE

willing to die for Christ.

Ephesians 5:25 says, *"Husbands, love your wives, even as Christ also loved the church, and **gave himself** for it."* These many people have given us an example of what it is like to give oneself for the church. I believe these people possessed the quality necessary to be a good mate and to stay a good mate. If necessary, they were willing to die for Christ. If you would not die for our perfect Christ, you probably would not stay with or die for a man or woman who is imperfect.

Romans 5:7 and 8 says, *"For scarcely for a righteous man will one die: yet peradventure for a good man some would even dare to die. But God commendeth his love toward us, in that, while we were yet sinners, Christ died for us."* Before you get married, realize whom you will be marrying — a sinner! When you say the words of the marriage vows, *for better for worse, for richer for poorer, in sickness and in health, to love and to cherish, till death us do part,* take these words out of the marriage ceremony if you don't mean them! Don't say these words at the altar and perjure your soul. Don't say, "I do," to what you won't do! The marriage vows are until death, UNTIL DEATH, **UNTIL DEATH**, not until you get sick and tired of the way the one you couldn't live without is acting! People of poor character do not keep their word.

Many of you who are planning to get married are unfit for marriage. Many of you who are married are marriage misfits. You wouldn't die for Christ; in fact, you won't even live for Him. We need, for the sake of lasting marriages in America, someone to have the character of a martyr. I am vowing to stay married. In fact, I will die to stay married! Americans dispose of mates like people throw refuse in the garbage can. Never get married with the thought of divorce as an option. Don't even use the word "divorce" in your vocabulary. We cut the word "quit" out of the dictionaries at our house. It might just be as good an idea to cut the word "divorce" out of your dictionaries.

Commitment until death is what I call upper-level commitment. Job 13:15a says, *"Though he slay me, yet will I trust in him."* In essence Job was saying, "I would be willing to let Him kill me." The truth is, very few would die for Christ. Husbands, I beg you to love your wives as Christ loved the church and gave Himself for it.

The Misconception of the Baptist Bride

God compares the husband-wife relationship to the relationship between Christ and the church. As of today, there is no bride of Christ. A woman becomes a bride at, and not before, her marriage. Let me give you a step-by-step account of what happens for the church to become the bride of Christ.

The word *church* comes from the Greek word *ekklesia*, which means a *called-out assembly*. Everyone who is saved will form a *called-out assembly* at the rapture — called out of this world to meet the Lord in the air. That *called-out assembly* then becomes the bride of Christ.

The Marriage of the Lamb takes place during the seven years that follow the rapture. *"Let us be glad and rejoice, and give honour to him: for the marriage of the Lamb is come, and his wife hath made herself ready."* (Revelation 19:7) The Marriage Supper of the Lamb takes place **after** the marriage — that's a reception.

There is no such thing as the "Baptist Bride." Remember that the Marriage of the Lamb takes place after the rapture. Only then will we be His bride.

Chapter 25

Character and Our Eating Habits

IN PROVERBS 23:21 THE BIBLE promises, *"For the drunkard and the glutton shall come to poverty: and drowsiness shall clothe a man with rags."* Matthew 11:19 says, *"The son of man came eating and drinking, and they say, Behold a man gluttonous, and a winebibber, a friend of publicans and sinners. But wisdom is justified of her children."*

As Americans, we live among many characterless people. As a result, we also live in a nation of people with very poor health. These two factors go hand-in-hand. A person of little or no character will not have the character to eat properly.

Are you familiar with the computer term, "GIGO"? It is an acrostic for "Garbage in, Garbage out." GIGO merely means that a computer can only print out that which has been programmed into it. In the same way, when we eat the wrong kinds of food, our bodies cannot produce the right type of energy. Therefore, Americans need to reestablish principles of right eating and proper treatment of their bodies. The following simple principles will be helpful concerning this:

1. We should always eat the kinds of food to keep our bodies healthy. The four basic food groups are essential for good health. Fruits and vegetables are important to your well-being. Drinking eight or more glasses of water daily is essential for good health. Choosing foods that use fewer preservatives will aid in health maintenance.

2. Don't eat too little or too much. Not a bite more or less should enter your mouth than what would be needed to help you to achieve ultimate productivity. By not eating enough, you will not have enough energy to do your work. By eating too much, you may slow yourself down as well. Do not allow excess weight to destroy your skeletal system. All the body systems — circulation, nervous, muscular, endocrine, etc. — depend upon the skeletal system for support. Once the skeletal system is damaged, your usefulness to God decreases.

3. Do not live to eat, but realize we eat to live. Our generation seems to think that we are to "eat, drink, and be merry for tomorrow we may die"; but we should actually eat, drink, and be merry for we have a work to do.

4. Do not waste food! Again, we live in a characterless society which throws more food in the trash than people in many countries will ever have to eat. This is a sin against God, as well as a sin against the person who provided the food.

5. Do not go shopping at the grocery store when you are hungry. If you shop while you are hungry, you will buy more than you need, and you will buy grocery items that you do not need. It is always wise to take a list that is prepared in advance and then have the character to follow that list. Purchase items that are necessary to good health.

6. Do not eat at restaurants too frequently. Not only is this a waste of your money, it is a waste of much-needed family time around the table. You will also find that most of these meals are not prepared in such a way that is conducive to good health.

7. Learn to clean your plate. It is a character flaw not to finish what you start. Many times we put larger portions on our plate than we can eat. We would be better off taking smaller helpings, then getting additional food if we need it. I believe that the old saying, "Your eyes are bigger than your stomach," must surely be true of some people.

8. Eat a good meal at the beginning of your day. By eating a good meal early, your body has an energy source upon which it can depend throughout the day. The word "breakfast" means literally, "to

CHARACTER AND OUR EATING HABITS

break fast." You are breaking the fast from yesterday's supper to this morning's breakfast. Break that fast with healthy food. No one starts a trip on an empty gas tank! It is best to start your day out right.

9. Be very cautious of eating before you go to bed at night. The purpose of your sleep is to rejuvenate your system. Your body needs to rest. If you eat before you go to bed at night, you are forcing your stomach and your digestive system to work throughout the night, therefore robbing your body of much-needed rest. You will find yourself very tired when you awake in the morning.

10. Don't eat excessively during your lunch break at work. To do this is to rob your boss of productivity. Many people are less productive after they eat than before they eat because their body is weighed down. Do not eat a bite more than necessary to increase your energy so that you can be as productive as possible.

11. Be careful of overeating at any testing time in your life. Students need a clear mind; therefore, they should be careful of eating too much when trying to learn. We should be careful of eating too much when going through spiritual testings. Making the digestive process undergo extra work will cause the mind to be groggy and dull.

12. Sometimes we need to fast and give up food completely for a planned amount of time. It is not necessary for one to remove food from his schedule for a prolonged length of time. One could fast for one meal or perhaps one day. There is no mechanical engine on the face of the Earth that runs continually for 60, 70, or 80 years without some type of breakdown. Most of us take better care of the engine of our car than we do our own body. Many of us work our digestive system our whole life without ever giving it a break. We would be healthier if we would let our digestive systems just shut down and rejuvenate. Unlike our car, a person cannot trade off his body for a new one.

We need character in the area of our eating habits. Utilizing just a couple of these 12 simple ideas will help to build character. At first some steps may be difficult to follow; however, saying "No!" to ourselves will help build character.

Chapter 26

Character and Our Money

IN I TIMOTHY 6:10 THE BIBLE says, *"For the love of money is the root of all evil: which while some coveted after, they have erred from the faith, and pierced themselves through with many sorrows."* Let me share some principles I have learned on how to handle money.

1. One should understand the importance of earning his money. We should give an honest day's work for an honest day's pay. Never should we be involved in gambling or stealing or taking advantage of someone. God set up a plan whereby we should earn our money.

2. We should attempt to save money for a rainy day. We live today as if there is no tomorrow. We need to realize that we are foolish if we spend all. Many people arrive at old age no longer able to work and have nothing at all set aside for themselves. There is nothing wrong with saving a little money; in fact, it is very wise to do so.

3. Give God a tithe. Malachi 3:8 says, *"Will a man rob God? Yet ye have robbed me. But ye say, Wherein have we robbed thee? In tithes and offerings."* The tithe belongs to God. If you do not give God one-tenth of your gross income, you are a thief. It is God Who gives us 100 percent of our increase. He commands that we give a mere one-tenth back to Him. I believe that God would have us to work with our money on a percentage approach. I believe our government could solve their tax problem if all people in all financial brackets would pay a flat percentage of their income as a tax.

4. Earn the money to purchase an item instead of getting the item and then trying to earn the money. We should work before we enjoy the benefits of work. Our credit-prone society will pay much money on interest charges because we want something today that we have not earned. If the cash is in hand, no interest will be paid, the product will be owned, and you will have earned the right to have it.

5. If you must borrow, have collateral. Collateral is something of equal value to the amount that you are borrowing. If you happen to default in paying, your lender could take your collateral, and your reputation would still be intact. Someone might say, "I have no collateral equal to the amount I want to borrow." If that is the case, then that person has not earned the right to own the item he is considering purchasing via credit. It may be that you just need to work harder and save to earn that item.

6. If you do borrow, repay all and on time. We are very inconsiderate in the area of our promptness in paying our bills today. If you cannot pay on time because of an emergency, call your debtor to let him know your payment will be late. If possible, go to see him in person. Then make arrangements to pay what you can rather than withholding all. Never abuse grace periods.

7. Do not be stingy with your money. When God blesses you with money, be willing to share the blessing with others. It all comes from God, and He could choose to withhold it from you just as you have withheld it from others who are needy.

8. Do not shop in places where you cannot afford to purchase the merchandise. We too often tempt ourselves. A husband should not drive his wife through an elegant housing division which could tempt her to want something more than they can afford.

9. Do not take advantage of your parents in the area of finances. Many people seem to think that because the lenders are their parents that it is not important to repay them. You are a thief if you do not repay a loan, whether it is to your parents or to a bank. Many times parents are forced to forgive loans because their children just assume the parents do not need their money back. Often a parent will be cautious in correcting an indebted child. The parent may feel somewhat responsible for helping to create this character flaw, seeing they trained this indebted child. No child should slap his parents in the face by demonstrating poor character in the area of repaying a debt to them.

10. Most of what you consider money problems are actually character problems. You need to get your spending under control. Never spend more than what you make. Your income should never exceed your outgo. This is simple to fix. Adopt the philosophy that if you don't have it, you won't spend it.

11. It is urgent that you stay organized in your finances. If you have a checking account, keep it balanced. If you have a savings account, watch it carefully and know where you stand concerning it. If you have debts, know when and how much is due. When you earn a paycheck, see to it that it is appropriately distributed.

Please answer the following questions: Would you rather have a $10,000.00 salary increase or the character to live on what you currently earn? Or possibly, would you like to develop the character to live on $10,000.00 less than what you currently earn? We seem to think the answer to our problem is to make more money. I wonder if the answer to our problem would be to develop more character.

Chapter 27

Character and the Importance of Finishing What You Start

THE BIBLE TELLS US that Jesus said in Luke 2:49, *"...How is it that ye sought me? wist ye not that I must be about my Father's business?"* Joseph, Mary, and 12-year-old Jesus had gone to Jerusalem for the feast of the Passover. *"And when they had fulfilled the days, as they returned, the child Jesus tarried behind in Jerusalem; and Joseph and his mother knew not of it."* (Luke 2:43) After leaving Jerusalem, Mary and Joseph thought Jesus was somewhere on the caravan. At first, they were not concerned. After looking for Him among relatives and friends, they determined He had been left in Jerusalem, so they returned to the city. When they got there, it took them three more days to find Jesus. When they did find Him, He was in the Temple sitting among the learned men, asking questions and astonishing them with His answers. *"And his mother said unto him, Son, why hast thou thus dealt with us? behold, thy father and I have sought thee sorrowing."* (Luke 2:48b) At Mary's question, Jesus answers, *"Wist ye not that I must be about my Father's business?"* Jesus was saying that He had some tasks to do. He knew He must **finish what He started**.

1. Organize yourself so that you finish what you start. If you want to be miserable in life, just start something and never finish it. I find that when I start falling behind with my work, it has a negative effect on my life. Since I know this about myself, I have already devised a routine solution. Let me share my method.

I go to my office where I keep all of my work. I take a piece of paper, and on that paper I write everything that I need to do. I then work on something on that list until I finish a task. I have a big, bold, black Magic Marker that I use to mark over the task I just finished. I choose every job on that list that I can finish quickly, and finish those jobs first. After I finish each task, I take my black Magic Marker and cross each completed job off my list. Those black lines give me a feeling of accomplishment!

Every time I cross out a completed job, I think, "I'm feeling pretty good about this day. Now I'm getting somewhere. I have made good use of my time!" Before long, there are more black marks on the list than there are tasks that I need to finish and ... I'm on top side again!

2. You should finish your schooling. Every child must enter school, so if you had to start school, finish school! However, our government, which asserts that a child of school age must go to school or be declared truant and subject to court action, says to rebellious 16-year-old teens, "Well, you are 16 now, you can quit high school." That is foolishness! You should never quit; after all, one of God's principles is that we ought to finish what we start!

If you have quit school, go back and finish what you started. Let me share a very personal example. My mom quit school when she was 16 years old, and she was miserable. When Mom became 21 years of age, she returned to school for her diploma. Can you imagine going back to school and becoming a sophomore again when you have been on your own? I have no doubt that it was tough for my mom to finish what she started. She has never regretted finishing what she started.

If you quit school and you are like the typical dropout, it will not be long until the welfare system is supporting you. I guarantee you that you will be miserable on the welfare system. Your self-esteem will be destroyed. Another danger of quitting school is being unable to find a good job. There is fast coming a day when a person must have a college education just to get paid minimum wage. I personally know people who have college educations who are unable to find jobs in their given fields of study right now.

If you started high school, **finish** high school. If you started college, **finish** college. **Finish** *whatever* course of study you begin no matter how long it takes you to finish.

3. If you get married, finish with the one with whom you started. The Bible says in Matthew 19:5 and 6, *"...For this cause shall a man leave father and mother, and shall cleave to his wife: and they twain shall be one flesh? Wherefore they are no more twain, but one flesh. What therefore God hath joined together, let not man put asunder."* When you got married, you started something, so finish what you started! Quite simply, that means you are not supposed to get a divorce. You can say, "But Brother Owens, my parents settled their problems by divorcing." I am not talking about your parents. I am talking about **you** never getting a divorce.

People today are making a mockery of marriage and divorce. Marriage is not a game little kids play; marriage is for mature people. Decide that when **you get married, you will stay married.** Never consider divorce to be an alternative. I promise you, you will be miserable if you get married and do not finish what you start. Sad to say, many more people will be miserable — the person you divorce, your parents, your children, and those who have invested in your life will all be hurt irreparably.

4. Do not start things that are not worth finishing. For instance, if you begin reading a book and find it has nothing of value for you, don't waste your time finishing it. There's nothing that says you have to finish an insignificant book. Use your wisdom!

5. Do not start listening to gossip; you cannot finish someone else's problem. Proverbs 14:6a says, *"A scorner seeketh wisdom, and findeth it not."* The Bible uses the word *"scorner"* as a description for someone who is a gossip. This verse teaches that when a person who criticizes another looks for wisdom from God, he will not find it. I am warning you: *don't you start something you can't finish.* Do not listen to a critic because there is nothing you can do to help the one being criticized. You probably do not have the wherewithal to help that situation. What you have allowed the critic to do is put a problem into your brain and into your heart that you cannot solve. **You cannot finish what you have started!** Don't spend time around people who talk disparagingly about others. You cannot solve another's problems;

you will do well just to care for your own!

6. Do not start a loan if you do not have the character to finish making the payments. We live in a society today where many think you get credit cards and write checks to enjoy yourself in life. However, I believe you are a thief if you owe anyone money and you are late one day paying it back. Do not borrow money unless you can afford to pay it back. Never begin a debt for which you cannot finish making all the payments.

7. If you started to live for the Lord, finish it. In John 19:16 the Bible says, *"Then delivered he him therefore unto them to be crucified. And they took Jesus, and led him away."* The Bible tells us in John 19:40 that Jesus was put to death and buried. In John 20:15 and 16, Jesus was not only crucified, but He was buried, and He was resurrected from the grave. When He was a 12-year-old boy, Jesus said, *"Wist ye not that I must be about my Father's business?"* Jesus was saying that He had much to do, and He had to finish what He started. The Bible gives us several accounts of when Jesus did just what He was supposed to do — *He finished what He started!*

So ought you to finish your Christian walk. Every Christian needs to finish what he starts in his Christian life. For instance, if you have been saved, that is not finishing what you started. Yes, you are on your way to Heaven if you are saved. However, the Bible says in Matthew 28:19 and 20, *"Go ye therefore, and teach all nations, baptizing them in the name of the Father, and of the Son, and of the Holy Ghost: Teaching them to observe all things whatsoever I have commanded you: and, lo, I am with you alway, even unto the end of the world. Amen."*

God says there are three things that ought to be finished in a person's life: (1) he ought to get saved; (2) he ought to get baptized; and (3) he ought to go and tell everyone how to be saved and teach them how to do what he did.

Let me ask you a question: Have you been saved but never baptized? You ought to finish what you start. Perhaps you have been saved and baptized. Are you telling others about Jesus? You should start doing what God has instructed you to do in His Word, and then finish what God directed you to do. **Finish what you start!**

"You cannot judge the character of a book by its cover. A book of good character will entice its readers to complete its reading. A book of great character will not only be read, but its principles will be lived by its readers. It therefore, in time, will be read by the entire world."

– Dr. Jeffery A. Owens
May 1995

MATERIALS AVAILABLE FROM OWENS PUBLICATIONS

Books

CHARACTER

MORE CHARACTER

PRACTICAL COUNSELING PRINCIPLES FOR CHRISTIANS
BIBLICAL COUNSEL AND HOW TO GIVE IT

THE ANT THAT MADE HIS BURDEN A BRIDGE
(A STORY COLORING BOOK)

CHARACTER LESSONS FOR CHILDREN (COLORING BOOK)

OBEDIENCE LESSONS FOR CHILDREN (COLORING BOOK)

BIBLE CLUB MINISTRY MANUAL (ENGLISH OR SPANISH)

CD Albums

MESSAGES THAT MOTIVATE

UNFORGETTABLE SERMONS

RED HOT SERMONS VOLUME #1

RED HOT SERMONS VOLUME #2

OLD-FASHIONED PREACHING

HOW TO BUILD AN ADULT SUNDAY SCHOOL CLASS

MARRIAGE—LIVING HAPPILY EVER AFTER

THROUGH THE OLD TESTAMENT

THROUGH THE NEW TESTAMENT

"...'TIL DEATH DO US PART"

TEACHING SUNDAY SCHOOL TEACHERS TO
TEACH SUNDAY SCHOOL VOLUME 1

TEACHING SUNDAY SCHOOL TEACHERS TO
TEACH SUNDAY SCHOOL VOLUME 2

CD Albums

    MESSAGES FOR YOUR FAMILY

    SERMONS OF ENCOURAGEMENT

    HELPING THE FALLEN

    SERMONS THAT HEAL

    PREACHING ON MISSIONS

    OLD-FASHIONED PREACHING

    LESSONS FOR LADIES

MP3's

    CHILD REARING (PLUS DVD BONUS)

    SOUL WINNING OR SOUL LOSING?

    BIBLICAL FINANCES

    PRAYER IS ASKING

    THE HOME

    WHAT THE BIBLE TEACHES ABOUT THE BIBLE

    BIBLE DOCTRINES MADE PRACTICAL

    PRACTICAL BIBLE LESSONS ON GOOD MUSIC

DVD's

    GET CRANKED UP!

    SOUL WINNING MADE SIMPLE

FOR MORE INFORMATION, CONTACT:
OWENS PUBLICATIONS
PO BOX 1597 • MARTINSBURG, WEST VIRGINIA 25402
(304)229-1338
WEBSITE: WWW.OWENSPUBLICATIONS.COM
E-MAIL: sales@owenspublications.com